Louise Baber

Snips and Snails

Snips an Sr

BY LOUIS

McGraw-HILL BOOK COMPANY, INC.

New York   London   Toronto

SNIPS AND SNAILS

Library of Congress Catalog Card Number: 52-8330

Published by the McGraw-Hill Book Company, Inc.
Printed in the United States of America

To my Godsons:

THOMAS EYRE THURESSON
MARK FREDERICK BIXLER
JONATHAN GARRETT DAUBIN
JAMES HARSH CORNEHLSEN
MICHAEL WEBSTER PEPLOW

Contents

CHAPTER ONE   SANDWICH IN THE EYE   1

TWO   SOUL SOLD   10

THREE   MALE ORDER   18

FOUR   THE OTHER SARDINES   30

FIVE   RELUCTANTLY TO SCHOOL   44

SIX   BOY CRAZY   56

SEVEN   SONS IN THEIR COURSES   65

EIGHT   FEATHERED AND OTHER FRIENDS   73

NINE   NOT CHEAPER BY THE DOZEN   81

TEN   TEN-O'CLOCK SCHOLAR   96

ELEVEN   BEAU GESTURES   108

TWELVE   MUSIC HATH POWER   118

THIRTEEN   AN HEIR AND A PARENT   131

FOURTEEN   THE LIGHT FANTASTIC   148

FIFTEEN   MEN OF LETTERS   165

SIXTEEN   A BIRTHDAY   183

SEVENTEEN   IN MEMORY   193

Snips and Snails

Sandwich in the Eye

L<small>ITTLE</small> did I suspect what I was grooming myself for when I used to sit up straight at table and eat my spinach like a good girl. I thought I was minding my Ps and Qs and my mother so I could have my dessert. But, actually, what I was unwittingly doing was nourishing my blood and sinew and building the Body Beautiful for sacrifice on the altar of Pedagogy. So help me—in my dewy innocence, I was growing up to be a schoolteacher.

At age nine, had I peered into a crystal ball and been warned of my fate, I probably would have foregone vitamins and surrendered to malnutrition and pale death. I knew a few schoolteachers. My set, known colloquially among local educators as "those brattish fourth graders," had a healthy respect for the ruler-wielding hierarchy. But certainly none of us entertained any serious intentions of emulating them.

But Nature has her way, as a wise biologist once said. He was sharper than he knew. Nature concocted the sex urge to take care of propagation and she contrived economic necessity to fill the teaching ranks. Prosperity had taken a powder when I emerged from college. For all my proud possession of a genuine sheepskin, I had no "career" aspirations at all and a similar amount of bucks in the bank. I only had job hopes

1

and they were few and frail and completely undiscriminating.

Although schoolteaching isn't contrived to gratify the gourmet's taste, it does provide three meals a day. In fact, if you teach boarding school at the bottom of a good deep depression, that's about all it does provide. Anyway, the hungrier you get, the more suggestible you become. I know I became so amenable to any proposals rife with vitamins that I even sank to accepting all invitations I got to teas. Which shows how far one can go in catering to the alimentary canal.

When Mrs. Peter Kensington Matthews II invited me to "a little tea," I was definitely delighted. I'm no snob. It was not so much the thought of the social feather in my cap as it was the thought of hors d'oeuvres in my stomach.

"How's about my wearing The Hat, Gigi?" I said to my sister. "I have been invited to the Matthewses' for cocktails. Or are you invited, too?"

"No," my sister said, "I'm proud to say I am not Gloria Matthews's type."

"Don't be smug," I said. "It's probably just that she heard we only have one hat and that it looks better on me."

"Well—anyway—congratulations," said Gigi. "Imagine Gloria remembering that she knew you when you were just Aunt Sarah's less attractive niece. Maybe we should buy a rose for the hat. The Matthewses are social register."

"Yep, I know," I said, "but you can get the social register at the library. I'm going for the groceries."

"Maybe you'll meet someone who will give you a job." My sister is the lovable type who carries a lucky penny in her shoe and believes in Kathleen Norris and the women's slick magazines. "Or maybe you'll meet a man."

"Or maybe they'll serve thick hamburgers for a change instead of Cheesy Weezies and dime-sized cold toast, spread with glup. Pull yourself together, Gigi, there are no jobs and all men are married or down at the Main Street Mission getting saved for the sake of a free meal."

My sister never aims for the nail's head but she often hits it unwittingly. I not only ate caviar that afternoon, I ate my words the next day. My sister was right in principle if not in dreamy detail. At the cocktail party I met a man—dark, handsome, and tall for his age—which was, alas, eight years old. And the next day I got a job—teaching school.

My feelings about children had always tended toward ambivalence. I had from time to time entertained the vague notion that I might someday produce a couple of nice, housebroken, curly-topped toddlers. I would name them something decorative like Michael and Melissa and as small fry they would pass platters at parties and grow up to be poets and adorn my old age.

However, when it came to evaluating realistically the offspring of my friends, I was somewhat less enthusiastic. I'd heard the opinion advanced that children are like avocados—the taste grows on you, but I'd nibbled very sparingly. Most of my acquaintances seemed to have a natural propensity for breeding brats.

And Peter Kensington Matthews III—imagine three of them!—was certainly a case in point. Nevertheless, it became apparent that Peter and I had a couple of things in common at that festivity—which it was my unsolicited opinion he was too young to attend. We didn't know anyone and nobody seemed specially eager to get acquainted with us, and we were both hungry. I ignored Peter as much as one can ignore a hurricane in a very crowded drawing room. But eventually, irresistibly lured by my charms, no doubt, he *made* himself felt. Playfully, shall we say charitably, but with forceful accuracy, he flung an open-faced sandwich my way.

I'll say this for his foolishly doting mother: she didn't condone his exuberance. "Tut, tut, darling," she reproved him. "We don't throw sandwiches at our friends."

"She's not my friend. I don't even know her," Peter explained sensibly enough. "Besides, it's not a sandwich. It's only got one side to it."

Gloria was telling Mrs. Spencer Fordham about the new astrologist she'd discovered and, of course, she couldn't be expected to prolong the discipline of her son at a time like that. "We won't throw any more sandwiches, will we, pet?" She let it go at that.

"You didn't throw none," mumbled Peter, and cagily didn't pledge himself beyond that.

His mother returned to Mrs. Fordham and the matter of major moment. But I wasn't busy—or I wouldn't be anyway as soon as I had swabbed out my outraged left eye which bore the full cheesy brunt of the attack.

"You're quite right, Tertius pet, I'm not your friend," I said in my most charming manner. "I'll be frank—being a woman, I can't throw quite accurately, but I promise you, much as I respect sandwiches, there's a one-sided, so-called, one coming your way. I always pay back my social obligations."

"You mean you're going to throw one at *me?*"

"Who else?" I cooed.

He pranced right over eagerly—the lovable little saber-toothed tiger. He diagnosed me a boasting braggart, bursting with big talk. With definite skeptical challenge, he tilted his freckle-spattered face up at me. "Let's see ya smack me one," he baited.

There was something almost appealing about his grin— with one gaping hole, front center, where he'd lost a fang —that almost distracted me from my purpose. But I pulled myself together and rededicated my life to Justice. Okay— I'll never darken the Matthewses' door again, I thought. So what—an agreeable enough fate. The food wasn't *that* good.

"Your Papa is paying for this, Peter," I said, "so we'll make it expensive. Close winken, dear." I plucked a particularly fancy concoction from the tray in front of me. "Well—here's caviar in your eye," I said. I would have loved to sink it smack in his bright brown little blinker—but a wave of tenderness attacked me. Instead, I carefully cleared his eyes—and smeared it, gluppy side foremost, into his left cheek. It was caviar to the four winds.

For one moment an expression of startled bewilderment possessed his face—or at least that part of his face not possessed by caviar. Then he yowled, but with sheer delight! "Oh *boy!*" He doubled his fist over another piece of ammunition. "Who'll we do it to now?" Conspirators—pals—soulmates—sandwich pitchers—that's what we were!

I pulled him down beside me on the sofa. I blotted him with my handkerchief while he attempted somewhat vulgarly to clean up his cheek with his tongue.

"Can't throw any more sandwiches," I said mournfully, as if the decision hurt me more than it did him. "People are starving all over the place, you know. Wouldn't be right."

He looked seriously thoughtful. Good heavens! He had principles! "Wouldn't be right," he agreed with compassionate finality. "I guess I better eat them so they won't be wasted." Shreds of nobility! Fascinated in spite of myself, I watched him toss hors d'oeuvres indiscriminately down his gullet by the handfuls. It would have revolted me if he hadn't been doing it for the Underprivileged.

But Petie and I had one moment of close spiritual communion. He spoke to me from the fullness of his heart out of the fullness of his mouth. "I hate all these stinkers," he announced soberly.

Rather than give the impression I was a "yes girl," I merely answered ambiguously, "Well—that's one point of view." But I did just barely squeeze his grubby fist, which happened to be resting in my hand at the time. If he wanted to make something of it, he had my permission.

The next day his mother telephoned me and said it was simply charming how well I understood children, entering right into the spirit of things with them. I embodied the sheer essence of the new psychology, if I recall the citation in its finest detail. "The new psychology" seems to change every year on the year. At that time—rather startling—it was, it seems, to bite a child back if he bit you. A sandwich in the eye for a sandwich in the eye. I was glad Peter hadn't bitten me. I've got a sweet tooth, sure—but my stomach is much too delicate to relish gnawing on little children. Besides— and the emotion rather startled me—I realized that I would not want to bite Peter because I remembered him with a strange tenderness. As my sister has often said to me, "You do go for the damndest men!"

"You were so quick—so instinctively right," Gloria practically cackled at me. She would have made a fine presiding officer in a hen house. "It's rare, my dear—such a God-given gift, if you know what I mean. I think children are guided by an occult hand to the people who understand them, don't you? Like Peter—picking you out of all that crowd yesterday. What if he'd chosen Madam van Vorst or Professor Harding? Oh, my dear, just imagine if he had!"

Gloria, I felt, was overrating Peter's aim and underrating his intentions. It was my secret suspicion that Pete had actually taken a bead on Madam van Vorst immediately following her delicate pat on the head and her perjurious observation that he was a "fine little lad."

"Yes," I agreed somewhat breathlessly, "I felt quite Legion of Honor yesterday. You could see everyone was simply livid with jealousy when that *canapé* was unloosed."

"Oh—you're laughing, aren't you? But really, it quite touched my mother's heart about Peter—*my* heart I mean, you know. He remembered you in his prayers last night. It was awfully dear really, so touching. Peter said, 'And God, skip Grandma this time, and bless the lady who heaved the sandwich.' "

Petie and heaven were in rapport, apparently. God skipped Grandma and blessed me. Although at the time, the blessing struck me as a gift horse whose teeth I felt inclined to X-ray. Gloria knew I needed a job. After all, I had said so as pointedly as I could without actually suggesting she fire Maid Mathilda and engage me.

"What better place for you, my dear—so in tune with youth and that sort of thing—than at The Oaks? They need a teacher for the little Acorn group—the eights and nines, you know."

Ominously it crossed my mind that dear little Petie was eight. He and the other little Acorns and I could face each enchanted day together.

"After all," Gloria clucked with respectful awe, "you graduated from *college*. Some special way, too, like *magna* something, wasn't it?"

She had me confused with an unpleasant cousin of mine named Marilyn who graduated *magna* something. I graduated by the skin of my teeth. But it seemed unnecessary to argue about anything as trifling as my intellect.

"Dr. Barrett is actually in town today—all the way from Prado Verde—that's where the school is. It just shows it was meant to be."

"Where's Prado Verde, Gloria?"

"Arizona—so much better because of week ends."

"Come again," I said. "What's that about week ends?"

"Oh—you know, better for the children. It's so upsetting to routine when they're close enough to come home every Saturday and Sunday. They get so tired and eat the wrong things. Prado Verde is too far away for that, but still close

enough to drive over from Los Angeles. I'll call Dr. Barrett.
He's the headmaster, you know. At the Ambassador, inter-
viewing students and parents. You probably know him, don't
you? But of course, you do, my dear—simply everyone who
is anyone knows Dr. Barrett."

"But, dear Gloria," I confessed modestly, "I'm not anyone,
you know."

"Well—he's a marvelous man, my dear, simply marvelous.
Terribly educated, like you. And not a medical doctor, you
understand—the other kind, you know—a Ph.D. So much
nicer, I always think—no night calls. Much happier for his
wife, if you know what I mean, but of course Dr. Barrett's a
bachelor. Oh, my goodness! I never thought of *that*—both
of you so smart and everything. He'll snap you up—for a
teacher, I mean. Grandfather Matthews gave the new gymnasium, you know, not that that would make any difference
to Dr. Barrett. He's much too high-minded for that sort of
thing. But it did bring us together, Dr. Barrett and me, I
mean, working on the plans. I designed the shower curtains
myself, with green fish—" Even Gloria has to breathe. She
paused to make a strangled gulp for oxygen.

"You do have a touch." I snatched my opportunity for a
pleasantry, while her chest rattled.

"Yes, I admit I do, my dear. I did the new wing on our
house, without a decorator. Even the man from Sloan's was
impressed. But what I mean about Dr. Barrett is that he respects my judgment. I'm quite deep, you know, and Dr. Barrett understands me. He admires me—my mind, if you know
what I mean."

I couldn't even imagine what she meant. But I did need
a job terribly.

"Well—I do covet a salary," I admitted. "I've gotten into
the hideous habit of liking to eat." After all, I could always

wear shatterproof ski goggles during the snack hour with the Acorns, I figured.

"That's settled, then. I'll call Dr. Barrett. Such a fine man and such a wonderful school. It's the best in the West and the children stay sun-tanned the year round—cunning. It's just like an Eastern school, with forms, you know. It's just for little boys, but still, it's like Groton, where Mr. Roosevelt went. Although I know an old Groton boy and he assured me that things like Mr. Roosevelt didn't happen there often. Only the nicest children from the best families are at The Oaks—that sort of thing. You'll love it."

I do not love "that sort of thing."

Nevertheless, authentically costumed in my cousin Marilyn's second-best schoolteaching dress, which she loaned me reluctantly—white dots on navy (her best one was blue dots on white)—I prepared to put my soul on the auction block.

"What do you think I should lie about, Gigi?" I asked my sister before I put The Hat on my nervous head for my crusade.

"The gymnasium sounds pretty solid," she said. "Cross your fingers and slap it on a bit about how cozy you are with the Matthewses. Also tell him how you just love children and have always wanted to teach."

"But I don't, you know."

Gigi got that other-world look on her face and passed down her intuitive prophecy. "You'll get the job, darling," she said. "And you'll just love it, particularly the kids. I feel it in my bones."

In retrospect, I'll say this for my sister's bones: they have it all over tea leaves, astrological signs, and crystal balls. I'd even stake my sister's bones against a Gallup poll.

CHAPTER TWO

Soul Sold

THE Ambassador Hotel in Los Angeles has always represented something wondrous to me. I remember when I was fifteen how envious I was when my sister, in a black-chiffon evening dress (short in front and long in back) with a white orchid on her shoulder, lit out for the Coconut Grove on the arm of a very handsome sporty spender. When I graduated from high school, I got there myself. Bedazzled, I wore my white-organdy graduation dress and went with a nice, bony boy who bought me a slightly droopy camellia from a street vendor and paid lavishly for three Cokes apiece so we could dance all evening in the Grove. We split the cover charge. It was bewitching. We saw Bing Crosby and lots of other beautiful people that we were certain were movie stars incognito. This was a long time ago, before restaurateurs pioneered the Beverly Hills frontiers.

Another kind of awe was generated when I was forced to approach the place alone and on foot, as I did the day of my interview with Dr. J. Treadway Barrett. The trek from the bus stop on Wilshire Boulevard to the entrance is so long and so emotionally shattering. It gives you too much time to speculate whether your stocking seams are straight and whether your slip shows, and you get a paranoid notion that you are the only person in all Los Angeles who cannot afford

10

a taxicab. Also, that day, I kept wondering wistfully who extracted the dandelions from the wide, spacious, immaculately barbered lawns around the Ambassador. Now a job like that was one I could tackle with my talents tied behind me. Schoolteaching was something else again.

My hands felt clammy. Not accustomed to wearing gloves —that was my trouble, I decided rationally. This Dr. J. Treadway Barrett—why should I be afraid of *him?* After all, he "admired Gloria Matthews's mind." I ought to strike him as a Danielle, come to judgment—yeah!

My appointment was for eleven-thirty. There were seven minutes to wait. In the lobby I relaxed myself for the interview by sitting on the edge of my chair, my spine rigid, listening to my heart beat. It couldn't be coronary thrombosis, could it?—not at my age.

"*I* before *E*, except after *C.*" A teacher named "Meanie" Morgan taught me that when I was eight. That ought to set the Acorns on fire. It was, alas, the only sound bit of pedagogy I had on tap.

What in heaven's name did headmasters ask prospective teachers? "What's seven times seven? Quick now! Do you have any bad habits? . . . Do you count on your fingers? . . . Do you split infinitives—yes or no? . . . Spell a few hard words for me."

And what in heaven's name did prospective teachers tell headmasters? "Seven times seven is forty-nine. I don't want to brag, Dr. Barrett, but I got *A* in Archery when I was in college. I've read all the works of Ellery Queen. . . . I'm bilingual—speak Pig Latin like a native. . . . *I* before *E,* except after *C.*"

Oh dear—maybe it would be better to win him with feminine wiles. But, alas, neither The Hat nor my unpleasant cousin Marilyn's second-best schoolteaching dress provided that kind of confidence.

"*I* before *E,* except after *C*. . . ."

What was Gigi's advice? "Lean on the gymnasium. Love children—love children—"

" 'The Children's Hour,' by James Russell Lowell—no, by Longfellow, Henry Wadsworth—is my favorite poem, Dr. Barrett."

"Grave Alice and laughing Allegra and Edith with golden hair." All three of them sounded like revolting little prigs. Why did Alice have to be such a sour puss all the time and what in hell was Allegra so hysterical about? As for Edith— the sneak—getting away with *anything* just because she had golden hair!

My favorite poem had better be about boys. "My favorite poem, Dr. Barrett, is that charming tribute to childhood by the good, gray poet John Greenleaf Whittier." Or *was* he the good and gray one? "It begins, 'Blessings on thee, little man' " —no, that would never do. Obviously The Oaks didn't covet the barefoot-boy trade.

At eleven-thirty on the button, I called him on the house phone. He said, "Come right on up to Room 504."

This seemed daringly irregular, but still, I decided schoolmasters probably had diplomatic immunity. If not, this at least would be a situation I could cope with more assuredly than I could with a question on "The Theory of Education at the Elementary-school Level." That was the sort of thing my unpleasant cousin Marilyn was always insinuating into a conversation.

Dr. J. Treadway Barrett greeted me at his door. He had an armful of white chrysanthemums.

"How do you do, Mr. Barrett." In my nervousness I clipped him of his degree.

"*Doctor* Barrett—Ph.D., you know," he corrected me. He scowled slightly. "I haven't finished arranging my flowers, but do come in anyway."

He proceeded to place his extravagant posies one by one in a large crystal vase, stepping back each time to squint his eyes at the effect he was achieving. He tapped one slim finger against his cheek as he frowned at the flowers. He was younger than I had expected, but obviously precocious. He looked like someone who had foregone frivolity years ago. He was a handsome man, if you aren't too partial to muscles. His hair seemed very blond in contrast to his complexion, which was as smoothly tan as a season-chaser's or a cautious long-term addict to an ultraviolet lamp. His ease of manner seemed a touch synthetic and his gestures had a studied grace.

"Do you think a large red one would be jolly in the heart of the arrangement?" he asked me finally. "What do flowers mean to *you?*" he demanded before I had a chance to give him my unbiased opinion about the heart of the matter.

I before *E*, except after *C*—*indeed!* I thought to myself frantically. "Roses are red, violets are blue. . . ."

He answered his own question, fortunately. "They talk to me," he announced, and tilted his head as if listening.

"Now—let's have a jolly good chat." He sat back in his chair and started poking some fine-odored tobacco into a pipe. I felt just about as chatty as a deaf-and-dumb hippopotamus and just as graceful.

I had the definite impression that J. Treadway was not an Englishman but that he regretted this shortcoming considerably. Still, there was no doubt a brief British breeze had once wafted over his speech—but it was no hurricane and had caused no impressive transfiguration. It had merely ruffled up slightly what was probably once a good, honest Indiana drawl. I decided with what proved remarkable clairvoyance that J.T. had probably attended a summer session at Oxford University, no less—certainly no more.

A beneficent seraph must have been assigned to me for the day. Something, anyway, prompted me to say, "You're

British, aren't you?" It was inspired. He was *hooked*, Matthews Sports Arena or not!

"By jove!" he said, and tapped his pipe, knocking out all the tobacco he had so carefully put in it, and stowed it into a tweedy pocket. "Curious your asking that. As a matter of fact, believe it or not, I was born right here in the U.S.A.—but I'm invariably taken for an Englishman. Dashed unpatriotic for me to look this way, what? Ha! Ha!"

Dashed smug— Ha! Ha! I thought, but after all, when you set out to sell your soul you can't be too fussy about haggling methods. I felt safer. After all, my schoolteacher disguise just might be as effective as his John Bull outfit.

"Well—unpatriotic or not, you do look like an English gentleman. Besides, I am a great admirer of the British." This, at least, was no lie.

He squinted at me in precisely the same manner he had squinted at the chrysanthemums. I interpreted this as a good sign, and I was right. "You know, I think I just might use you," he said, with only slight reluctance.

It looked as if I were going to be able to conceal my guilty secret after all. He seemed completely uninterested in my lurid past, with its dishonorable record of misspelling and infinitive splitting.

"That would delight me, Dr. Barrett." But strictly from hunger!

"We've never hired a woman teacher before." He said it firmly, as if hopefully determined that things would never again come to such a pretty pass. The thought of a job filled me with heady rapture. Dr. Barrett obviously wasn't similarly transported at the prospect of engaging me, however. He paused for a long, impressive moment of silence. He cut into me with a deeply penetrating stare intended to snip a specimen off my cancerous soul. He pulled out his pipe and

stuck it mid-point below his clipped blond mustache. He
bared his teeth, while he chewed on the pipe stem. They were
flawless teeth. No nicotine stains. I wondered vaguely if the
pipe were ever fired up.

"Now, the Matthewses think highly of you. Fine, discriminating people, the Matthewses. But I am a man who makes
up my own mind. Mrs. Matthews says you need a job rather
badly. I hope you can find one—but obviously in selecting
teachers I cannot be influenced by need. Do you know what
does influence me?"

"No," I admitted breathlessly. I hoped fervently that it
wasn't the candidate's Philosophy of Education.

"What I *must* know is why you want to *teach*. It is perhaps
the most important question I ask a prospective staff member.
Can you understand that?"

"Yes, I can, very readily, Dr. Barrett," I agreed. It was a
good enough question, but in answering it I would certainly
have to cross my fingers. I couldn't confide in J. Bull Barrett
that I was simply on the prowl for a piece of bread—and I
didn't even care whether it had a buttered side.

"Well, Dr. Barrett." I had to feel my way cautiously. "I
want to serve some real purpose in the world." How much
better Gigi, with her heart in this sentiment, could have said
it! I crossed my fingers just to be on the safe side of Providence.
"What more satisfying role could I hope for than teaching
the young? Molding the little minds, if you know what I
mean." I reminded myself of someone. It was unnerving to
realize that I sounded exactly like Gloria. "It would humble
me, but at the same time exalt me, I know. Besides—" I bade
Honor farewell; recklessly I flung myself into the spirit of the
thing and sealed my infamy—"I love children."

Barrett leaped to his feet. He shook hands with me in the
manner of a lawyer congratulating a shady client who had

skidded on some very thin ice but had finally been acquitted by a drowsy jury. "You are hired. That's all I wanted to hear you say."

Frankly, however, I don't think it mattered too much what I said. I suspect that neither my perjury nor my credentials were very persuasive. In the final analysis, Dr. Barrett selected me, I am convinced, because he was behind the eight ball and at the crucial moment I happened to be behind the eight ball with him. Some of the parents had been putting the squeeze on him to add a woman to his all-male teaching staff. That he was, by and large, compliant with parents was fortunate for me. That he had postponed this particularly unpleasant acquisition until the eleventh hour was even more fortunate for me. He had already announced over his own signature that a woman was to be added to the faculty that fall. It was already September first and he had still left unaccomplished his reluctant duty. The timing of my appearance was fortuitous and, of course, it did no harm at all that I came under the Matthews banner. But the most decisive circumstance in my favor was the fact—which I discovered later—that to Barrett, women were women and he took a dim view of the entire sex. I suspect that he actually believed that grabbing blind netted the same results as careful selection. Either way, you got a woman, and the former course at least had the virtue of cutting down contacts to the minimum. Since I was the first female to be interviewed, I got the job.

It was as simple as that. It wasn't even a chicken feather in my cap—but I didn't realize how unornamented I really was. I was as ecstatic as the Queen of the May.

I was, in fact, so intoxicated with my incredulous rapture that in my nervous eagerness to get out of the room before Dr. Barrett changed his mind, I tripped on the rug. Frantically, I reached out for ballast and got a half nelson on the vase of chrysanthemums. The flowers succumbed to my attack. What they said to Barrett I don't know, but they flung themselves petulantly all over the floor, while the water washed down the front of my borrowed schoolteacher's dress. In my abject horror I clung to the uptilted vase.

"Oh—" I gasped. "Oh—"

"Give me back the flower bowl, if you please," said Dr. Barrett firmly, as if he expected me to slip it under my skirt and flee. That was just the sort of thing he anticipated in women, I suppose.

"Oh—" I gasped again, the horrible thought crossing my mind that maybe now that his flowers and I were on fighting terms, he might snatch back the job, along with the vase. "About the job . . ." I faltered, still holding the vase as hostage.

"I'll explain your duties when you arrive at Prado Verde. You had better go now. You're all wet."

With this flattering accolade ringing in my ears, I phoned Gigi from the Ambassador. "Come on downtown, darling. I'm your rich relative now. A big chalk-and-eraser tycoon. I'll spend fifty cents to have Marilyn's dress pressed and then—"

"Oh, mercy—" interrupted Gigi. "Is he *that* kind?"

"Perish the thought! I'm afraid he isn't *that* kind at all. We'll spend my four dollars and ninety-five cents for a new hat, and you put in a buck of yours and we'll go see the new Shirley Temple picture at the Paramount. From now on in, she's my favorite actress. I just love kids."

The hat was a bad investment. Slick operators in Arizona wear sombreros. But seeing Shirley Temple was sound indoctrination. She turned out to be the unanimous choice of my little schoolboys for "The Girl I Would Least Hate to Be Marooned Indoors with on a Rainy Saturday."

CHAPTER THREE

Male Order

MY FIRST impression of the school was that it was set down in the dead center of nothing. Arizona often gives that misconception to the newcomer. To feel the beauty and admire the subtle brutality of Arizona, you have to live there through a whole cycle of seasons. Until I went to The Oaks, I had a very casual attitude toward the "Great Out-of-doors." It was a place all the healthy, hardy people went to eat dry sandwiches and get mosquito-bitten and return wiser and considerably worse for wear.

I felt that I had conquered Nature for all time when I learned ten birds, ten trees, and ten flowers to get the Big Pine Badge at girls' camp. Arizona's brand of Nature isn't something that can be snubbed with a perfunctory "How pretty." Arizona is all things to all people—from the Valley of the Sun to the Snow Bowl at Flagstaff. Nature in Arizona is a tantalizing changeling who charms you with a flowered spring, threatens you with a feverish summer, floods you out in the rainy season, and snows you in come February—according to whim and altitude. She's wanton—but wonderful!

The school buildings were adobe—dun-colored, low, earth-clinging, and flat-roofed. Flat roofs and adobe are really impractical in the colder areas of the Southwest, and in winter

Prado Verde was cold. Adobe washes away and flat roofs can't take an overload of snow. But certainly a school of the caliber of The Oaks was pledged to sacrifice efficiency for artistry. Besides, the Indians and the early Spanish settlers in the Southwest built with adobe (there was nothing else to build with) and anyone with a nice regard for tradition must do likewise. So, although pitched roofs are practical blessings when fifty-two inches of snow descends in one season, flat-roofed adobes are still favored by the Rich, who can afford them, and the very Poor who can't afford anything else.

My father lent me the money to buy a secondhand Model A Ford which would be my proud own at the end of ten five-dollar installments. I arrived two days before term opening, looking almost as bushed as my buggy after the hot trip across the desert.

Dr. Barrett assigned me a garage immediately. There weren't enough garages to go around, so the masters with the worst-looking vehicles got them. More ornamental cars had the questionable distinction of sitting out in the driveway month on end.

Upon my arrival, Dr. Barrett gave me a quick briefing on curriculum and dealt me an eight-card hand of three-by-five filing cards. They were all "wild" cards—every one a joker! On each was a name with descriptive high lights, supposedly designed to orient me to my charges. Here were the lads whose "bright promise," as Dr. Barrett put it, I was assigned to keep polished. Reading over the notations, I realized with resignation that every card had the words "Tuition Paid" scrawled across the bottom. Regretfully, I abandoned the whimsy that perhaps the little boys would not show up, and I would get an eleventh-hour reprieve, and could go home and reform and start a new life. The sparse paragraphs did nothing to alleviate my mounting anxiety. Every word merely fortified my theory that little boys had been extravagantly flattered by the lyricist who defined them as made of "snips and snails and puppy dogs' tails."

Nervously I shuffled the cards.

PETER KENSINGTON MATTHEWS III. Age 8. Somewhat domineering. Tends to argue. Leader. Good in athletics. Family gave gymnasium. Mother feels grades should be higher (correct). Tuition Paid.

HOMER WILLIAM CURTIS. Age 9. Highest I.Q. in school. Day boy. Father professor on sabbatical leave from New England college. Homer sometimes depreciates faculty. Poor in athletics (correct). Tuition Paid.

ROBERT MILLBANK LENNOX. Age 8. Slow learner. Good in athletics. Stomach upsets. Untidy. Won't wear underwear unless coerced (correct). Father may give school new tennis courts if Bobby does better next term. Can't read well nor spell (correct). Tuition Paid.

JAMES TRACEY TRAVERS. Age 9. Average student. Parents exceedingly rich but vulgar. (Child's middle name in honor of popular moving-picture actor that mother admires.) Jamie close friend of Peter Matthews (discourage—Matthewses disapprove). Table manners and language crude (correct). Interested in sex (correct). Tuition Paid.

KEVIN CLARK. Age 8. Mother Mrs. Byrne-Masterson, four times divorced. Mother wants Kevin to learn to play piano, improve in sports, and gain weight this year. Has unpleasant nervous habit of pushing at his cowlick (correct). Tuition Paid.

LAWRENCE WILSON DRUMMOND. Age 9. Father mining engineer in remote area in Mexico where there are no schools. Family find it a hardship to meet even adjusted tuition and are constantly anxious about Larry's welfare. Make excessive demands for lengthy reports, etc. Boy cooperative and bright but causes subtle dissatisfaction among peers by constant talk about family life at home. Mirrors parents' notion that boarding schools are only for children who live too far removed from day schools (correct). Parents also insist that Larry see his sister every week—student at Shadow Creek. Interferes with schedule (discourage). This boy may be dropped—not good pay and considerable inconvenience. First tuition installment paid.

WINTHROP STANDISH BANNISTER. Age 9. Fine old family. Mother complains he came home from school last summer saying, "Aw crap!" (correct). Sometimes wets bed (correct). Tuition Paid.

JEFFREY HAMILTON CARRUTHERS. Age 8. New boy. Son of president of Roco Oil Company. Mother says he bites fingernails (correct). Tuition Paid.

Correct—correct—how did I correct nail biting, enuresis, reading disability, allergy to underwear, sex instincts, crude table manners, admiration for family life, athletic clumsiness, bad spelling, blasphemy, and "pushing at cowlick"—whatever under the eclipsed sun that meant! Naïve dewey-eyed innocent that I was, I had always assumed that all that teachers corrected were papers.

"As you can see," Dr. Barrett said, "there are one or two small problems in your group."

"Yes, I see," I agreed.

"Just a minor challenge to make your job more interesting."

"Yes indeed." There lay the gauntlet, and even knowing my scabbard was empty, I picked it up.

My quarters were in Kirkland Hall, the newer of the two dormitories. Actually, the building was supposed to retain the modestly anonymous title of "Dormitory II," until that hazy day when Johnny Kirkland graduated. But Johnny's progress was slow—so slow in fact, that at times his scholastic status was dangerously tottering. After six years at The Oaks, aided by much tutoring and some pedagogical charity, Johnny had labored through four grades. His father presented the dormitory to the school as a matter of expediency. The gift was the last desperate gesture of a loving parent who believed in Education for his children at any cost. In Johnny's case, that was a pretty penny. Mr. Kirkland himself shifted policy in midstream and started calling the building "Kirkland Hall." He felt, no doubt, that it was probably sound procedure to keep everyone reminded of his investment. To prevent any possible miscarriage of his intentions, he agreed to burn the mortgage on the building the day Johnny got his diploma. He was determined to get Johnny through the eighth grade before he turned sixteen. So was everyone else. A boy who shaved was an inconvenient anachronism at The Oaks.

The bathroom schedule in the mornings was designed to accommodate only the unblemished chin.

My suite was comprised of a living room, a bedroom, and a bath. Convenient for my supervisory duties, it was located at the end of the long corridor off which opened the dormitory rooms reserved for the eight- and nine-year-olds. My living room had very little furniture in it. This was because it must also serve as commons room for the Acorns, and the school had an unsound theory that children just love to sit on the floor. There was a nice, hard, straight chair for me and a sturdy desk on which to grade papers. There were two uncomfortable, hideous, heavy Spanish Mission chairs, tinged with Grand Rapids, which, I discovered, would accommodate approximately six eight-year-old boys per chair. Oddly enough, they preferred such crowding to sitting on the floor. It was more challenging. The rugs were of the scatter genus, Navaho, and skidded into grotesque heaps when trod upon carelessly. They were definitely throw rugs. They threw the unwary, providing much simple, clean fun for the Acorns.

A large fireplace, banked on both sides with books of the *Junior Encyclopedia* ilk, dominated one wall. Sprawled in front of it, the little tads were supposed to loll through a thousand and one nights while I warded off destruction by making like Scheherazade.

Off the living room was a cubicle, playfully called a "bedroom." It would have been spacious enough if it hadn't been for the bed. It wasn't that the bed was pretentious. It was, as a matter of fact, a singularly narrow cot with a slight spinal curvature, but it took up all but sidling space. A one-hundred-and-ninety-pound man had uncomplainingly occupied the box the year before, I was informed. But I filed that myth away with the George-Slept-Here legends.

The bathroom was small and had only a shower, no tub. This was reasonable enough since no time was allotted on my schedule for luxurious, bath-salty soaking. The shower was bereft of a tap handle on the hot side. Apparently the one-hundred-and-ninety-pounder was a virile sort who yanked off the fixture with his bare hands, having no truck with warm water. I borrowed a pair of pliers from Windy Bill the school horse wrangler and handy man (alleged), to use in turning on the valve until that nebulous "first opportunity to fix it" came upon him. For six months, I carried the pliers to the bathroom with me. By that time, I was so handy with plumbers' tools, I fixed the faucet myself.

From my sitting room, I had a wide-window view of the cactus-cluttered landscape, five of the fourteen oaks, and the full grandeur of the San Francisco peaks, the twin, white-topped monuments that lorded it over the lesser mountains at whose feet the school salaamed. The two peaks, in the vernacular of the school, were "Old Bare" and "Old Baldy."

I approved the view, but the object that really brought calm to my uneasy soul was the piano in the living room. I decided that it would compensate for whatever ill fortune flogged me. I can play two Chopin preludes and half a Beethoven sonata in a manner highly satisfactory to myself—if to no one else. I was very happy about the piano. I tossed the contents of a suitcase onto the bed, skidded across the room on a rug, and started fondling the old upright Steinway. It was in tune.

There was a metronome sitting in silent and deceitful innocence on a shelf. My goodness, when had I last seen a metronome? Not since I was twelve certainly! That should have been the tip-off. But with naïve glee and no premonition of doom, I ripped through the hardest of my preludes.

The faculty supposedly had arrived for two days of orientation, but the boys were not due until Sunday. The dormitory was so echoingly empty, I didn't even think of closing the door, a humane gesture I usually make prior to my moments musicale. Just as I was banging into my finale, I smelled smoke. It came, I discovered, from an unappetizing pipe which protruded from the rugged but nicely hewn face of a tall loose-jointed male creation. He apparently had barged right in, without benefit of invitation. A music lover, no doubt. Actually, even had the door been closed, he was precisely the type of character who would have walked in without knocking. There was something arrogant and untrammeled about him that no mere door could frustrate.

"I *thought* maybe you played the piano," he said. "Speak when you're spoken to."

"Well—really, give me time—I play a bit, but scarcely in the manner of Mozart, man or boy," I said inanely.

He didn't put up any argument—the cad! "No, that's obvious—but I can see you *like* to play, anyway. You look self-satisfied doing it. You're loud, too. I'm glad I picked you for the piano."

"What do you mean—picked me?" I asked.

"I had it moved in here at my own expense. Tuned, too. Nothing too good for the little woman, I decided. I told Barrett you might like it. After all, I had it in my room all last year."

"That was awfully kind of you, really. Are you a master here?"

"Yes—I'm Joseph Hargrave, chief arbiter of the Pines. Teach, too—English, Math, History, Tennis, Football, Nature Study, Second Swimming Coach, First Riding Master, Plastic Arts, First Aid, Woodwork, Gardening, Calisthenics, *et cetera*. We turn our talents into all channels here. No idle time hanging tempting and empty on our hands. Maybe you can palm it off on Wallace. He's new, too."

"Palm what off?"

"The piano—if you get bored with it."

"Oh heavens, I won't get bored with the piano," I assured

him. "It will be a great comfort to me. It was most generous of you."

"Not exactly generous—although I assure you I *do* do generous things sometimes. I was glad to—damned delighted. And although I don't usually regret my sins, I'm sorry. You look a good sort. Right purty. You mellow me. I apologize for giving it to you."

"What do you mean?" I peered at him. Too bad I thought, that such a handsome concoction was so mentally handicapped.

"You'll find out soon enough. *O tempora! O mores!*" He twisted his mouth offside and whispered the sinister words through his teeth. "They prac-tice here," he informed me. "Now you know."

"Who?"

"The little Liszts. *Do-re-mi-fa-sol-la-ti-do.*" He sang it. "Some of them are beyond scales, of course. They're onto a little number called, I think, 'Birdie in the Spring.' And one exceptionally talented genius can get through two pages of the "Minuet in G." Of course, he begins over—and over. It's a bit tantalizing, but diverting."

"When do they practice?"

"Oh—just mornings—and afternoons, and evenings up to bedtime. The violin boys come in occasionally to join forces with the piano. Ever been in a boiler factory when they've doubled up on the riveting crew to get out an emergency order?"

"Hardly."

"Then, of course, you have no intelligent basis for comparison, but take my word for it, the boiler factory is a symphony. But they don't like doing it to you—poor, put-upon little bastards. Of course, you can play the piano whenever you want to in-between times. But not after bedtime, you understand. Might wake up the small guys. And not before breakfast. They sleep then, too. And not after lunch. That's rest period—for the boys. You'll probably be correcting papers then anyway or just sitting and glorying in the miracle of uninhabited space. And the hour after dinner—that's study time. You'll supervise. And Sundays—there's chapel in the morning and stray-kith-and-kin visit in the afternoons. Of course, if you don't bathe, you might play during the hour before dinner? Do you bathe?"

"It's a silly conforming habit I've fallen into, but I'm thinking of giving it up. You seem to have omitted Saturday from your blissful account of Our Happy Week."

"Satan's Uncle! So I did. Saturday is fascinating. We divide them up and take them to town for haircuts. We herd them in and out of drugstores where they squander their allowances on comics and chocolate bars. Then the *good* little boys have lunch at the hotel and go to a movie. Like Westerns?"

"Just what do you have against me?"

"Nothing, now that I've seen you. You're not exactly what I expected Barrett to pick. I had you doped out as more utilitarian—a touch more tweedy and flat-soled, spewing hairpins in your wake and losing your glasses. But then, Barrett didn't pick you, did he? You're Matthews."

"Nonsense! Dr. Barrett makes up his own mind. He told me so himself."

"So he does—about what tie to wear each morning. But don't let it bother you. I'm a Smedley man myself."

"And who is Smedley?"

"Smedley's a trustee, but I have the edge on you. I spring from intellectual influences. Smedley is a college president. You're just money. But we mustn't be snobbish, just because it's the trend here."

"You're an unpleasant character, aren't you?"

"I try to be—but the boys like me. They'll like you, too. They're odd that way."

"Well, I don't care whether they like me or not. I don't like them."

"That's what you think now, Angel Face. You'll like them all right. Tear up the cards Barrett gave you. You can't write down these little guys. I have a feeling about you. I suspect you'll be standing right beside me in faculty meetings, shouting down the opposition. You and I are going to like the boys together."

"Don't call me 'Angel Face,' if you please, Spatter Brain. Is there friction here?" It was easy to see that there was going to be some between this Hargrave and me and, curiously enough, the prospect was highly exciting.

"Don't call me 'Spatter Brain,' if you please. Call me 'Joe' or 'Darling' for short. Friction? I don't think that's quite the word for it. It's the environment. It's just that in an isolated boarding school, the faculty members get pushed in on each other. It's like canning a bunch of sardines alive. The space is limited. You won't notice it at first. It's only when your fins begin to cramp. Long about Christmas you'll sell your soul for a can opener."

"My soul's in hock right now. But why do you teach? With your talents I just bet you could get ahead in the world as a ditchdigger or something."

"Oh, stop, you silken flatterer. I bet you say that to all the boys. I'll tell you why I teach—and listen closely because this is the rarest *honest* reason you'll ever hear. I like it. I have my discontent, of course—you know, Me and Socrates and the Pig. Teachers are a fiercely hating bunch. There are three types—those who begin about mid-November to hate the boys; those who begin hating the faculty; and the ambidextrous kind who hate both, and hate the dogs and horses, too, just for good measure."

"Who do you hate?"

"I'm a special type. Basically, I'm a parent hater. You're

the same formula. That'll be two of us. Naturally, I'm not much for the faculty either. It's pretty lonely hating the parents. Most of the masters *love* the parents. Why shouldn't they? Our parents are the 'Best People.' Besides, it pays off pretty well at Christmas in a simple sterling-silver sort of way. Some of our parents have yachts, too. Ever try to hate a man with a yacht? It's damned hard, but you can do it, if you put your mind to it.''

"I'm as broad-minded as the next person. I wouldn't hold a yacht against a man.''

"Me neither. I never let it influence me. I even gave Tim McNeill an *A* in Math and his father owns a 48-foot mahogany-lined, gold-accessoried cabin cruiser, complete with movie stars. That shows I'm democratic. He got plenty of *A*'s but I'm the only master who gave him an *A* in *spite* of the yacht.''

"My, you're just *wonderful*, aren't you?''

"See—what did I tell you? You and I think exactly alike. But it embarrasses me to have my charms discussed in my presence. There's a faculty meeting in ten minutes. We get briefed for the year's operations. Now, as an older man—I'm twenty-eight, you know, old enough to be the father of your children—I want to give you some advice. Watch out for Munsey. His mother was scared by a Greek statue when she was carrying him, I think. But don't be misled by his chassis. Now take me: I may be cut on more simple lines, but I'm more your type. Simple living, high thinking, heart of gold—you know, salt of the earth. I'll buy you a Yale lock for your door. He'll have no truck with Yale. Harvard man. I'm a Yale man myself. This is going to be a lovely year at The Oaks. The trees are going to be full of singing birds.''

I was suddenly terrified—not of Munsey, but of schoolteaching. "*I* before *E,* except after *C.*" It certainly wasn't much ammunition.

"At this point, Joe, I'd quit teaching at the drop of a hat.''

"You can't quit something you haven't started. At the end of the year, you'll buy a hat just to toss back in the ring. But maybe I won't let you work after we're married. Would you like to marry me?"

"Thanks, but I'm not the impetuous type—give me forty or fifty years to think it over, will you? I'm still young."

"Well, a girl can't be too choosy these days—but I won't rush you. Leave us go to the faculty meeting."

The Other Sardines

FACULTY meetings were habitually held in the headmaster's study. With the exception of a couple of plushy guest
rooms, coveted by two ill-housed masters, but meticulously
reserved for rare overnight visitors, the headmaster's study
was the show place of The Oaks. Here the best foot in its
shiny boot was thrust forward. The carpet on which many an
uneasy youth was called to shuffle his clumsy shoes was Ori-
ental. The furnishings were English antiques—most inappropriate to the high Spanish flavor of the architecture, but
excellent ones nonetheless. The fact was never avowed but
gently implied that these delicacies came from Dr. Barrett's
ancestral home. The implication also included the hint that
the ancestral home was in Surrey or Sussex rather than South
Bend, Indiana. The paintings were good water colors, but
somewhat pallid for my taste. One wall was entirely devoted
to portrait photographs of individual boys and to group pictures of serious-looking graduation classes and intense riding
teams, whose steeds were none too well lined up for the
take. Always, there were lavish bouquets of fresh flowers on
desk, table, and mantel. Depopulated, the place smelled somewhat like a lady's boudoir from which a pipe-smoking roué
30

had just fled. It was a pleasant enough room, but for some reason it always seemed slightly indecent to me.

Dr. Barrett certainly fancied flowers, there was no doubt of that. Apparently, however, only the most exotic blooms talked entertainingly to him. He had a standing order with a Los Angeles florist, and every other day the bus driver deposited a box, along with some underbreath blasphemies, at the school door. Dr. Barrett spent an hour every day arranging them charmingly in silver and crystal vases. I got to be quite a flower lover myself at The Oaks. But my proud taste, as it developed, ran to drooping, short-stemmed bouquets of wilting wild flowers, plucked off the range north of the athletic field and presented by the loving but grubby hands of my admirers. I spent five minutes daily arranging them charmingly in old Kraft cheese glasses. Mine talked to me, too—of my little friends who paused long enough in their play to pull up by the roots or pluck off at the heads the bright purple or yellow blossoms that tint the vast spaces of the Southwest in the rainy season.

The headmaster's study was like an excellent stage-set of a headmaster's study. And the faculty were like characters dreamed up by a diabolical playwright who was perverse—or stupid—enough not to provide them with any good lines. If that show hadn't been the real thing, it would have folded on its first curtain.

Joe led me by the hand to the meeting. I felt suddenly grateful to him and forgave him for the piano.

"Gentlemen," he announced, "I give you the Lady."

There was a shuffle of feet and seven men arose from their chairs. I had always wistfully imagined that it would be wonderful to have a roomful of handsome men hanging on my every word. However, when it happened, it was a bit unnerving. Maybe the trouble was that they weren't uniformly handsome. There was no doubt which one had been condi-

tioned by the Greek statue. In my comparison with the tall,
muscular, curly-topped Munsey, the other men looked like
old sepia prints competing with technicolor.

"Please don't stand," I said. "I expect to be around a long
time and you mustn't set any regrettable precedents for gal-
lantry."

Dr. Barrett took over. "I think you are wise in offering us
a gentlemanly retreat from the amenities. I'm sure you plan
to be one of us." He cleared his throat but it sounded sus-
piciously like a cover-up device for a sigh. "So, masters, as
soon as each of you is introduced, you may be seated. Now,
dear Lady, this gentleman is Mr. Frane, our Latin master."
Dr. Barrett gestured toward the most elderly of the group. Dr.
Barrett had a physical grace that enhanced his incontestable
but cold good looks. *"We* all call Mr. Frane 'Roger,' although
behind his back, the boys, I understand, have given him the
sobriquet of 'Old Baldy'—after our majestic mountain, no
doubt." The laughter was a bit undue. I caught on quickly
that Dr. Barrett expected his witticisms to be accorded emphatic response.

"You can see for yourself why they call me 'Baldy,' " said
Mr. Frane. I could see for myself. "Besides, I want you to
know they call me that to my face, or should I say, my pate?
And I like it."

I was glad he liked it. He looked like a nice, inoffensive little man, somewhat harassed and certainly nearsighted. His
spectacles were thick, and mended on one side with neat
patches of adhesive tape. Mr. Frane loved schoolteaching.
That was because he loved Latin and there's nothing much
you can do with Latin but teach it. His attempt to resuscitate
the dead languages was a conscientious dedication. He needed
a new suit badly.

"Can't grow a crop on barren soil, huh, Frane?" The coiner
of that classicism was Munsey.

It was apparent that Barrett admired Munsey. He was like the flowers and the furniture—a perfect collector's item of its kind. "Munsey here's our strong man." Barrett put a matey arm around the iron shoulder. "Handy if you need any trunks moved." Everyone laughed—a jolly crowd. Munsey squinted his eyes at me in a manner obviously intended to set my cells swirling.

"Maybe he'll let you feel his muscle. He lets the boys," Joe said.

Dr. Barrett ran through his gamut of expressions until he found one sufficiently vituperative, which he bestowed on Joe. I decided that Smedley must be a very important influence indeed.

The dark, nervous, thin young man clutching the box of Kleenex was Marcus Carson. He always sniffled his way through faculty meetings. He might have been forgiven for sinus trouble, a permanent head cold, or a broken nose, but his damp affliction was a most ill-chosen allergy. Flowers were intolerable to him. Barrett regarded the sniffles as a personal affront. Withal, Carson was almost as stable a commodity at The Oaks as the trees themselves. He owned and leased to the school half a section of the land that comprised the campus. Moreover, at least five of the oaks were rooted in his land.

He was much too retiring to bait Barrett openly. Still, he was crafty enough to mention casually from time to time within the hearing of reliable talebearers that a startling offer from a big mining company or a chain of restaurants had been made for his property. His reasons for not snapping up the golden fortune dangled before him were always high-minded and self-sacrificing. He couldn't bear the thought of The Oaks bordered on the north by unsightly machinery— or worse yet, threatened with an evil dance hall to whose bright lights and lurid cacophonies the innocent schoolboys might drift and fall prey.

I liked Carson. It was always gratifying to me to see such a mild hand so upper. Besides, only tame flowers bothered him—in fact, I always had a psychiatric hunch that his onsets stemmed from environmental, rather than botanical, causes. In any event, he could inhale my drooping lupine with immunity. He set the multiplication tables to music which seemed to me a significant contribution to pedagogy.

"And this fine young chap is our other newcomer, Mr. Craig Wallace." Young Wallace was twenty-one, just out of college, and anxious not to be noticed—a difficult feat since he was sizable, though not quite so flashily packaged as Munsey. He was teaching for a year, expecting to hoard enough money to go vagabonding. On the basis of my own abandoned hopes along those lines, I figured roughly that, with careful budgeting, he just might save enough for a bus ride to Phoenix by June.

"How do you do." He acknowledged the introduction with becoming blushes. "We're both new, I guess."

Here was someone more nervous than I. It calmed me. It was easy to see he'd been hunting for a hollow tree, too. "That's right," I agreed. "We'll have to stick together."

The thought seemed to comfort him somewhat. Or maybe it was merely that he was vastly relieved when attention was withdrawn and directed toward James and Jorgenson. Dr. Barrett introduced them as a pair.

"This is James and Jorgenson," he announced, as if presenting some rather dull matched twins whose individual identity he had long since abandoned in confusion. They sounded like a couple of soft-shoe vaudevillians or partners in a wholesale meat-packing business. James and Jorgenson were always lumped in this manner. They were about the same age, thirty-two or so, but they certainly weren't alike physically. One was tall and thin, with an Adam's apple, and one was short and fat, with no neck to speak of. Capable and conscientious though they were, their usefulness fully recognized, still to Barrett they were identical aggravating thorns in his side.

This was because they were married. Not to the school, as was Barrett, and he would have gladly condoned bigamy—but to women! Dashed inconsiderate, and unnecessarily biological. It required readjustment of living quarters and special consideration on assignment of evening supervision hours. It added two mouths to be fed—and heaven knows how many more, the way things were plunging headlong to a pretty pass. As an embarrassing topper to all the inconveniences that Holy Matrimony inflicted on Dr. Barrett, Mrs. Jorgenson, with indelicate animal zeal—or just perversity—became pregnant. It was a difficult crisis to face, but Dr. Barrett met it stoically. He simply ignored the whole process.

Mrs. Jorgenson's shifting contours were ignored by no one else, however. Her linear metamorphosis was discussed freely among the boys. Whenever the headmaster appeared, however, they became as stonily mum as a bunch of gossipy women suddenly interrupted by an innocent child from whom the facts of life must be concealed.

Mrs. Jorgenson, so Joe told me, prayed every night for a male child. She preferred girls, as a matter of fact, but felt her husband's professional future at The Oaks depended on her not raising the female population by so much as one very small statistic.

"There is one more master who is not here this evening. That is Fielding Newcomb. Mr. Newcomb has been spending the past month with the McNeills cruising along the coast of Baja, California. The McNeills, I might mention, for the information of new faculty, are one of our finest families. Tim McNeill is form leader for the Pines—a splendid lad, typical of our best achievement."

I had already discovered that we not only had Acorns at

the Oaks, we had quite a few other horticultural phenomena. The Acorns were not even the half of it. There were the Yuccas, the Junipers, the Spruces, and the Pines. Each year new names were voted by the forms, making for an intramural condition of utter confusion. The boys had gray-flannel blazers with the insignia of their branch of Nature embroidered on the pockets. Their lesser loyalty was for the blazer pockets. Their greater loyalty was for The Oaks. "Oh, Mountains fair, Oh, stalwart Oaks. . . . We bring our loyalty. . . . And sing with voices free. . . ." They sang the Alma Mater with loyalty and voices free, but not nearly as loudly as they sang, "She'll Be Comin' Round the Mountain," and "Hector, the Garbage Collector."

"May I offer you a bit of sherry?" This, I discovered, was part of the incorruptible ritual of staff meeting. Dr. Barrett had established a prudent compromise with the demon alcohol. Unwilling to risk the censure of those parents whose code rigidly prescribed that all schoolteachers teetotal, he outlawed hard liquor on the premises. On the other hand, although he didn't want to imply that when unleashed he was a rowdy tippler, there were parents who admired good two-fisted drinking masters. Dr. Barrett hit upon sherry and balanced it neatly on the two horns of his dilemma.

He made quite a fetish of his wine and could—and too frequently did—give a detailed history of sherry that was thorough and encyclopedic. The British, it seems, recognized sherry as one of the truly civilized drinks long before the Revolutionary War. And what was good enough for the British was good enough for Barrett.

He served only the best imported Amontillado, the periodic gift of a grateful parent. He always delicately passed his glass beneath his nostrils and sighed pleasurably before sipping. Some of the more impressionable masters imitated his gestures.

Poor Wallace, apparently confusing the amber liquid with a short snort of corn, tossed it down his gullet in one gulp. It was an unfortunate start for Wallace.

"Now, let's all settle down and have a good talk," Barrett said. "Cigarettes? Personally I don't see how anyone with discrimination can thoroughly appreciate the flavor and aroma of a good wine with a cigarette—but here—" He passed a hallmarked silver box which contained exotic Turkish blend, gold-tipped, monogrammed cigarettes. Five hundred of these expensive, bad-tasting insults to Virginia were presented to Dr. Barrett on indiscriminate holidays by Kevin Clark's mother, Mrs. Byrne-Masterson. She was a divorcee, temporarily at liberty.

Everyone, of course, brushed the very thought of cigarettes aside, except Joe. He scorned the handout, however, in favor of a Lucky from his own pocket.

"Now, gentlemen—*and* Lady—" He bowed in my direction. "We are on the challenging threshold of a new school year. These are troubled times. No one knows what lies ahead economically and socially. Communism threatens America, Europe flounders in unhappy confusion, and even here at The Oaks, for all the peaceful serenity of the place, our problems are as complex and paradoxical as those the whole world faces."

I alerted my ears—the likes of this I had never heard.

"You see the grim shadows as well as I do. The depression threatens the financial stability of our parent group—the very lifeblood of our existence."

Hargrave poked me. "Our parents, you know, carry their plasma in their pocketbooks," he whispered to me.

Dr. Barrett frowned, but continued. "This is the nature of the dark pall that hangs over us. But we must carry on— hew to the line. We must continue to bring the richness of health and culture and learning to our young charges. At the

same time, we must keep them free from those disquietudes
that trouble adult minds. It is our trust to preserve childhood's heritage—happy freedom under the wise and kindly
hand of discipline. But—I caution you, economy *must* be
practiced this year." Here, apparently, was the full flower of
his thinking.

"I cannot cut salaries. That would be unthinkable. A well-
paid staff is a happy staff." Everyone looked a bit uneasy.
Recalling the monthly figure quoted me, the staff probably
wasn't explosively ecstatic. "So—to avoid the possibility of
cutting faculty stipends, or more dire, even cutting the faculty,
I am asking all of you to watch the smallest expenditures this
year. I hereby appoint you all the royal guards of the ex-
chequer. Bear down and pare down."

He paused while we appreciated his epigram.

"That's good, sir. And you're right—dead right. We're the
world in miniature right here at The Oaks." That stupefying
giant, Munsey, was heard. "But what I'd like to know is, does
this mean that you won't approve my requisition for new
baseball bats and hockey sticks?"

"Not at all. I refer to such modest economies as saving the
ends of soap, turning off unnecessary lights, watching the
thermostat, and so on. The healthy, body-and-character-
building activities which you so ably direct, Munsey, are the
bulwark of our program at The Oaks. Knowing your sanity
regarding such license, I place no boundaries on the athletic
budget."

"Thanks, Tread, for your confidence." Munsey dropped
his head slightly in humble modesty, or I suppose that's what
it was.

"However, it has occurred to me," Barrett went on, "and
I'd like everyone's absolutely frank opinion regarding this
possible shift in policy, that we might encourage boys to
provide more of their own equipment. This comes to my
mind at this moment merely because we are speaking of

baseball bats. I do *not* regard this as an economy proposal, but rather as a sound device for character building. I think it would give the boys a beneficial sense of property to own their own bats and hockey sticks and a valuable sense of responsibility to care for these items themselves. Even group equipment—basketballs and footballs—might well be provided by individuals. It would encourage generosity—sharing with the group. Take Peter Matthews—if he owned a basketball and carried it to the gymnasium and offered it for all the boys to enjoy, it would bring out something essentially fine in Peter."

"Better take someone else, Barrett," Joe suggested. "Peter, you know, lets the kids use his *gymnasium,* although so far his generosity hasn't brought out anything essentially fine in him. Poor, perverse little duffer, he doesn't need any more possessions. He needs a quiet heart on which to rest his head."

Why, Joe Hargrave, the two-crusted pie, had a custard filling! It began to appear that the symptoms of mid-November were upon us prematurely.

"As is frequently the case, Hargrave, you deliberately confuse the issue. I merely used the first lad who came to mind as an example."

Joe ignored the rebuff. "Teddy Lane ought to provide the basketball. It would salve his soul to have a possession to share."

"Hargrave, you know quite well that Teddy Lane cannot afford extras. He's a scholarship boy."

"Sure, I know. That's why the basketball would help him. He can't even treat to Cokes. He never has anything to give the boys, besides a little help in arithmetic. Besides, this isn't an economical measure—this is a device for character building. Right?"

"That's what prompted my idea." The headmaster was simmering.

"Okay—so I move the *school* buy the basketball and slip

it to Teddy Lane so that he can lend it to the boys for the
sake of his character. Pride in good grades will carry a normal
eleven-year-old only so far."

"Mr. Hargrave, you are, I trust, sincere, but you are mis-
guided. You tend to scratch the surface. Teddy must never
be allowed to confuse his own financial status with that of
the general run of our students. That would be unfair to his
parents who sacrifice a great deal to keep him here, even
with the substantial aid we allocate."

"Hell—Teddy's paid off, with interest. He's yanked the
scholastic level of this school up by its bootstraps, and without
the precocious bigotry of that intellectual child snob Homer
Curtis. Is it all right with you if I buy Teddy Lane the best
damn basketball on the market and give it to him?"

Barrett was always palliated by the presence of a possible
donor. "Well, of course, Hargrave, if you want to do something so generous, I'm sure it would be greatly appreciated
by the boys. He's a fine, intelligent little chap." Barrett left
himself wide open. Joe delivered straight on the button.

"You don't feel, then, on second thought, that it would be
unfair to his parents?"

"Oh, *dry* up, Hargrave!" Munsey snarled. His face was
distorted with rage. It was not a nice sight. "Get Teddy the
blasted basketball—and I'll see that every kid here owns a
bat and hockey stick. We'll buy them wholesale and sell them
retail in the school store."

Barrett's momentary nervousness didn't quite conceal his
approval of Munsey's master mind.

"Gentlemen, let's drop this controversial matter. I think
we're agreed in principle, aren't we?" Heads bobbed. "We'll
settle the details in committee. On to other pressing con-
siderations. I want, first of all, to recapitulate some of our errors of last year—so that we may mold them into our growing wisdom."

He recapitulated.

Out of it all, one depressing revelation came upon me. I, an inveterate toast-and-coffee breakfaster, was going to eat oatmeal every morning and, what's more, politely smack my lips over it.

This was the essence of what Dr. Barrett called "Table Spirit."

"We are always urging the boys to show Table Spirit," he said. "We ask them to clean their plates and eat the good, nourishing food placed before them. But we, too, must show Table Spirit. Some of you, I have regretfully observed, urge food on the boys that you yourself do not choose to eat. This stimulates dissatisfaction with the board—which is, as you know, the best provided by any school in the West. We must be fair-minded if we are to be the examples incumbent to our Trust. Let's eat our spinach. Let's eat our oatmeal. Let's show Table Spirit, too, by doing cheerfully—and for our own good—what we demand of our boys."

"You said it!" chimed Little Sir Echo Munsey, who had a vulgar appetite anyway.

"And let's be on time at meals, please. And remember to check on personal hygiene at breakfast. Teeth, hair, nails, and ascertain if all at your table are wearing underwear. Watch Bobby Lennox particularly. His mother is most distressed over his grooming. Now—any questions?"

"Is it true that you are adopting a new textbook for my course in Ancient History?" Mr. Frane was the first master besides Joe and Munsey to loosen the cat from his tongue.

"I am, Roger. I have studied thoroughly a new work that seems to me a great improvement over the text we have been using. It is going to delight you."

"Well, I *like* Breasted. He's always seemed satisfactory to me."

"Baldy, old boy," Joe interrupted, "we *must* progress. If

you hang on to Breasted, you might be tempted to use last year's lesson plans, and what would you do with all that extra time? Moreover, be sensible. A new text is profitable for the school store. No competition from overly penurious boys peddling secondhand copies. The adoption of new textbooks, an established policy of this school, nets us a pretty piece of added income *annum* after *annum*. Be practical, Baldy. Be progressive, man. 'Ancient Times' have changed."

"Hargrave is our bitter wit." Dr. Barrett addressed me directly for the first time, in an attempt to break up the continuity of my breathless fascination. Apparently Mr. Frane had a new textbook, for Dr. Barrett carried the subject no further. Instead, he launched into his planned techniques for meeting the invasion of parents and boys on opening day.

It sounded something like an assignment of battle stations for a hopeless last stand against an overpowering enemy. "Remember, we're all in this together." He proceeded to outline strategies.

"Don't forget," he warned, "Mrs. Bannister is disturbed about Winthrop's language to the point where she may change schools."

"She'd do better to change husbands," Joe said. "Winthrop got those colorful words rubbed off on him before he arrived here and most of the lurid lingo the other Acorns use occasionally they borrowed from Winthrop."

"I question that. Mr. Bannister is a very cultured gentleman from Boston."

"You'd be surprised at the vocabulary that has penetrated Boston," Joe said.

"No matter—all I'm saying is keep every boy who might conceivably be capable of saying 'crap' away from Mrs. Bannister on opening day. And please take occasion to mention that the Corbetts and the Densmores, both new families, are old New England stock. I think it would be excellent for

Mrs. Bannister to meet Lance Markham. He's always so well groomed and well mannered. Mention that Lance is a good friend of Winthrop's."

"Well—he *isn't* a good friend of Winthrop's." Perversely Joe continued. "Lance Markham says no bad words—not above a whisper anyway—but he's got a headful of bad thoughts, and Winthrop, for all his language, is as uncontaminated as a newborn kitten. Larry Drummond is Winthrop's best friend, and he couldn't have a better one."

"Larry sometimes says 'crap' I might mention," Dr. Barrett announced firmly as if he were denouncing an international spy ring.

"And Lance Markham says 'I'm charmed to meet you' and cheats on examinations and climbs up to peek in the bathroom window when Mrs. James is bathing," Joe said.

"It has never been established that Lance was the boy Mrs. James saw at the window. She couldn't identify him conclusively."

"No," Mr. James put in his quiet word. "However, Dr. Barrett, he's the only boy who ever asked me if my wife's operation was for appendicitis."

"Lance plans to be a doctor, you know." Dr. Barrett frowned at everyone. "I think we've carried this matter far enough. Now, let's just relax and hear about vacations. More sherry?"

James stole a quick glimpse at his watch and shook his head in mute answer to Jorgenson's quizzical raised eyebrows. The Jameses and the Jorgensons liked to get in a quick rubber of bridge on those rare evenings when the men didn't have dorm duty or study-hall supervision.

But no one ever left faculty meetings until they were over. They were over when Dr. Barrett dismissed them.

CHAPTER FIVE

Reluctantly to School

THE environment and trappings of many occupations create a distinctive odor. A blindfolded man with an average I.Q. and standard olfactory accessories could probably recognize a print shop, a bakery, or a garage. Most of the so-called "professions," however, are pretty thoroughly scrubbed and disinfected. With the exception of the medical profession, with its carbolized aroma, I expect I couldn't pick any of them with my nose. But schoolteaching is the anomaly. I discovered it's a veritable potpourri—it reeks.

The sum total of the odor is the result of careful blending and aging of many ingredients—chalk dust, floor wax, furnace oil, damp corduroy on a rainy day, socks overdue at the laundry, apples, pomade slapped lavishly on a humiliating curl, the leathery smell of an old catcher's mitt, polliwogs in jars of green water, peppermint drops and young perspiration. I don't contend that, bottled, the essence would have any commercial future—certainly it wouldn't unsettle Chanel or bankrupt Bellogia. But exposed to it over a period of time, I progressively hated it, tolerated it, and—so help me —eventually grew quite partial to it. It's not a hazardous scent. One sniff won't unleash the baser passions. But, in its own modest way, it does have that subtle power, the prime

44

purpose of all perfumes, to stir the emotions. I suspect that even when I am a feeble and toothless old crone, if I should get a sudden nostalgic whiff of wet shoe leather and corduroy pants, faintly laced with licorice, I will automatically start a dreamy recitation of the multiplication tables—paralleling the old battle horse who kicks up his aged heels at the blare of a bugle.

But little did I suspect on opening day at The Oaks the existence of such a scent—let alone that I would ever be titillated by the elixir. This emanation isn't apparent on opening day. It reaches high fetor about mid-May when summer heat and unseasonable summer rains intensify its illusive components.

Opening day in a boarding school disavows any kinship with all other, mundane dates on the school calendar. It has a pleasant reek of its own like unto no other day in the year —even Commencement. It smells fresh and fragrant and deceptively wonderful. Fresh paint, floor wax, cedar-scented polish, fresh-cut grass, flowers, the delicious aroma of a specially impressive roast in the kitchen oven, and the blend of mothers' perfumes and fathers' shaving soap and good cigars, and the young, soapy smell of recently dunked small boys. Neither the school nor the schoolboys are ever quite as fastidiously tidy as on opening day. Mud quickly mars floors and gray-flannel jackets get tossed into the corners of closets along with cowboy boots and sweat shirts. Also, you can lead a boy to water but you can't make him soap—unless you stick a rod in his ribs.

The main lounge of the school was a fairly mundane room, usually cluttered with magazines and sedentary play equipment and smelling not unpleasantly of juniper smoke from the faultily dampered fireplace. On opening day, however, it was dignified with rigid order and enhanced with bouquets of fragrant flowers and a beautifully and abundantly arrayed tea table. The tea table was so placed that it concealed the "delicate condition" of Mrs. Jorgenson, who had been "honored" by Dr. Barrett with the privilege of presiding over the urns. Mrs. Jorgenson was, in fact, a prisoner for the afternoon, for the table had been so adroitly arranged in a corner that she could not escape without having the whole barrier picked up and moved first. Dr. Barrett had trapped her neatly. It was, from his point of view, politer than asking her to remain in her quarters. Projecting his own dim view of propagation, he felt sure the parents wouldn't approve of the "shape she was in." Mrs. Jorgenson spent a miserable afternoon, during which her hostility toward Dr. Barrett increased in direct ratio to her painful urgency to leave her post of duty, if only for a few minutes.

Everyone else in the lounge seemed to be in a state of frenzied transit. Faculty, all assigned to maneuvers, mingled with parents and boys. I was prominently displayed by Dr. Barrett to the parents who had favored the addition of a woman to the staff, and completely ignored otherwise. The whole place had some of the aspects of a battle station, with the milling troops marshaling for a major *Putsch*. Certainly Dr. Barrett performed like a campaign manager. He was at his superb best on opening day. He fancied himself, I suspect, as a blend of Lord Louis Mountbatten just before a tactical triumph and Sir Sacheverell Sitwell in a drawing room. This was modest underevaluation.

He was an amazing synthesis—all things to all people. Dr. Barrett always referred to the parents as the "Lifeblood of the School" and he had apparently typed and labeled a sampling from each, and perhaps had even had a swig of a transfusion. Anyway, he had his classifications at the tips of his nicely manicured nails. His approach to each parent showed a fine-line discrimination that a diplomat could envy.

Hargrave told me that Barrett achieved this Art by sinister pharmacology. "Barrett's got bloodstained copies of both Dun and Bradstreet and the social register locked in the bottom drawer of his desk," Joe insisted. "Under cover of midnight darkness he slips into his study and uses the pages of these books like magic litmus paper. He drops parents' blood on them—the coloration gives him a full analysis and cues his behavior."

Certainly his formula seemed faultless. He awed the ill-educated with his erudition. He frightened the naïve with his aloof sophistication. He matched the casualness of the secure. He gave the beautiful women the impression that he thought them intelligent. The intelligent women he managed to make feel beautiful. He could even behave humbly to satisfy the compulsively powerful.

With the boys he was more standardized, but so were they, and his technique with them was equally effective. He managed, even with his much-repeated lines, to express his unique pleasure and fresh joy at the sight of each boy. They all called him "sir"—a title of respect used in addressing all masters. He called them by their surnames.

"How do you do, sir?"

"How do you do, Mansfield?" He patted the boy on the back and conveyed subtly the impression that here was the *one* for whose arrival he had been breathlessly watching at the window.

"Nice vacation, Mansfield?"

"Oh, yes, sir."

"Glad to be back, Mansfield?"

"Oh, yes, sir."

"And so am I, Mansfield, most awfully glad that *you* are back."

All afternoon boys and parents spewed out of family cars and Munsey met trains with the school station wagon and collected boys in bulk lots—the ones whose parents were too busy to bring them.

A few boys were delivered by chauffeurs; and Jamie Travers, a shamed nine-year-old, showed up in the custody of a governess. He tried to pretend she wasn't with him, of course, but when that didn't work he attempted to pass her off as a relative, a touch of democratic deceit that would have horrified his parents, who were very proud of having achieved a governess.

"Who's the dame, Jamie?" Bobby Lennox demanded with no tact.

"Oh—*her?*" Jamie looked puzzled as if he'd noticed the woman for the first time. "Oh—well, she's my aunt, see—but she's going on tonight as soon as she unpacks me. Her name's Miss Benson."

Miss Benson was a good sort and tried to make herself as inconspicuous as possible. Jamie's parents were convinced he was the object of kidnaping plots and they never allowed him so much as a moment alone, although they themselves avoided his company as much as possible. But someone always accompanied Jamie wherever he went. One custodian signed him over to another, like a registered package, and almost as impersonally.

Jamie was probably the happiest boy at The Oaks. This was because, in spite of the plush in his home environment, the school gave him the only secure pattern of living he had ever experienced. For nine months of the year he felt safe. He explained it with more simplicity. As he said to me once, "I like it here, because there's people to eat with."

The halls resounded with boys' names—first names, nicknames, diminutives. Boys' names are wonderful—they sound like boys. Tony, Andy, Bill, George, Alan, Peter, Rickey, Kevin, James, Jim, Toppy, Jeffrey, Whitey, John, Jack, Fishface, Winthrop, Timothy, Fatso. . . .

There were two definite patterns adopted by returning schoolboys in hailing old friends. There seemingly was no approved middle course.

One approach was for two summer-separated pals to fling themselves at each other with wild shouts of incredulous joy —as if each had fully expected some catastrophic disaster to have destroyed the other during vacation. Equally popular, and equally emotion-packed with delight in reunion, was the stony, silent approach.

Larry Drummond, a charming nine-year-old, talked to me constantly for half an hour about the ecstatic moment when he would once more see "my friend Winthrop." "My friend Winthrop," he bragged, "is the swellest guy in this whole school—see—in the whole *world* Winthrop is the swellest guy, and he's my best friend." I remembered with a qualm that Larry, who supposedly said "crap" was to be kept away from Winthrop Bannister. Quietly I plotted to betray the well-laid plans of Dr. Barrett.

Winthrop, his mother later testified to me, had been similarly anticipating reunion with Larry. The Bannisters finally arrived.

"That's him," Larry whispered to me. "That's Winthrop."

The two of them stood and stared at each other and then turned their eyes away as if the spectacle were untenable. They hung their heads. They kicked at the rug, and Larry leaned down and scratched his ankle. They behaved like a Republican and a Communist forced to share a jail cell.

Finally, Larry mumbled "Hi," but he gave the impression that speaking was a concession he made reluctantly.

Winthrop, thusly challenged, said, "Hi."

"You back here now, Winthrop?" asked Larry.

"Yep," said Winthrop. "You back here, too?"

"Yep," answered Larry. "That's a silly tie." He reached over and pulled it out of Winthrop's vest.

"You quit that, you big—you big old crazy," said Winthrop. "Yours is silly, too." He pulled out Larry's tie. Oh dear— I cased the place quickly with my eyes. Mrs. Bannister was providentially over by the tea table with Dr. Barrett being introduced to Lance Markham.

"Crap!" said Larry, and I shivered. Larry hit Winthrop and Winthrop hit him back. It was the only way to achieve physical contact and still maintain their masculine pride. Then they smiled warmly at each other.

"Let's us take off these silly ties," proposed Larry.

"Yeh," said Winthrop. "Let's us do it." Sharing such revolutionary and noble dedication, they walked off together.

"Gee—Winthrop!" I heard Larry say. "Gee-jus!"

"I'll say!" agreed Winthrop. He put his arm around Larry. This was brotherly love at its best. Still, it did occur to me that perhaps I'd better try to improve on the Language of Love.

The school on opening day had a certain resemblance to a railroad station just before traintime. The principal differences were that all the passengers looked prosperous, tea was served, and there were no yellow cabs.

However, the same breathless activity and the same psychology dominated the atmosphere. Luggage—mostly by Mark Cross—was hoisted about and the full gamut of station farewells was run through. Embarrassed public kisses were exchanged. The tender dropped a few tears. The stout-hearted flung their falsely cheery phrases. "So long, fella— have a big time." And there was the inevitable restless male plucking at the feminine elbow. "For God's sake, let's get going. Let's get the show on the road."

Also there was a counterpart of that typically railroad-station impasse, when the good-bys have been more than adequately rehearsed and the irritating conductor still doesn't

call "all aboard." To fill the empty gap—too small for vital
communication but large enough to be a yawning vacuum—
parents, particularly mothers, dawdled desperately. They
plucked at their son's ties; brushed back unruly hair from
long-suffering brows that would have tolerated no such en-
croaching familiarity at home; and offered last-minute, trifling instructions about writing to Aunt Jennifer and watching out for cold snaps. The air hummed with reiterated extol-
lation of "Goodness," that indefinable elusive virtue so highly
and so monotonously recommended to children and so rarely
defined.

"Be a good boy" . . . "You'll be mother's good boy, won't
you?" . . . "I know you'll be a good boy" . . . "Try and be
a good boy. . . ."

"Yeh" . . . "Aw, Mom, sure" . . . "Yes" . . . "I'll be
a good boy" . . . "I will" . . . "I will" . . . "Sure
thing. . . ." Piping voices made their empty pledges as
agreeably as roll-call responses.

Like most departing travelers, the boys were eager to be
rid of their well-wishers and get on with the trip. "You can
go now if you want to" was the tender sentiment that vied
conversationally with the wholesale commendation of Goodness.

Only those poor, forlorn first voyagers, the "new" boys,
exposed the unsteady heart. With a great parody of fearless-
ness, they strutted their synthetic unconcern. But at the end,
they clung to the door handles of cars and babbled incoherent
inconsequentials to their departing kinsmen, postponing as
long as possible the painful severance from the familiar.

The first heart whose unmooring I witnessed was Jeffrey
Carruthers's. This launching created such imposing waves in
the area that my own stability was ripped from its anchor.

As befitting respect to the school's "Lifeblood," a random
delegation of faculty usually escorted all departing parents

to their cars. Joe, Warren James, and I happened to be the
convoy to the Carrutherses'. Jeffrey, a sturdy, dark-eyed, eight-
year-old, put on a fine performance of sophisticated acceptance
of boarding school. And Mrs. Carruthers bestowed her first-
born on the altar of Education with no Niobe-like symptoms.
Serenity certainly seemed to have a firm seat on the situation.

But suddenly as the big black Cadillac started slithering out
of the driveway, Jeffrey's controlled inner agony burst its
dikes. "*Wait!*" It was a full-throated wail. He turned his head
briefly toward us to explain himself. "Forgot to tell my mother
something awfully important." Even his prideful effort
couldn't conceal his desperation. He sprinted down the driveway.

The chauffeur slowed down and a rear window was lowered in respect to Jeffrey's falsetto, trumpeting his final in-
telligences. "Don't forget—" Frantically, he searched his
tortured mind for a major issue. "Don't forget—"

"Don't forget what, Jeffrey? Mother has a dinner engagement in Phoenix, you know. What is it, dear?"

"Don't forget—" His voice dropped to a chirping lamenta-
tion. "Don't forget to take care of my horny toads. . . . Remember, don't let anyone get into my stuff while I'm gone.
. . . *The horny toads!* They're in a box on my window. . . .
They'll miss me. . . ."

A careless kiss was tossed to him off a white glove. The
gravel under the wheels sounded a frenzied finale as the car
gained speed. Jeffrey took a few limping steps in pursuit and
then he stood in the middle of the driveway, his head tilted
to fit into the curve of his raised arm. Slowly, in the rhythm
of doomed fatality, he waved his uplifted hand. No one waved
back. The horny toads might miss him. . . .

One of his bare, sun-browned knees beneath his gray-flannel
shorts was plastered with white adhesive tape. It crossed my

suddenly unhinged mind that I would never send a little boy of mine away to boarding school if he had a sore knee—*never!*

There was a faint alien stirring inside me—which my feminine psyche defined on the first rumble. Egad—I thought, here is the kiss of death for my smug complacency. My unsuspected maternal instinct was as cooingly alive, I discovered, as if a fluffy pink bundle of toothless charms had just been thrust into my arms by a satisfied midwife.

"Oh, dear heaven!" I sighed. "Why didn't I take up cheerful work, like mortician's assistant? The poor, poor infant—his knee hurts." This was the most minor footnote to the tangled thoughts and emotions inside me. I was poverty-stricken for words. I ruffled my feathers and unfolded a wing like a fluttery-hearted hen, to offer shelter.

Joe restrained me. "Hold on, Cup Cake, you don't *like* the boys, remember!" He grabbed me by the arm.

"Hold on *yourself!*" I snarled at him. "I *love* the boys—damn it!"

"Still—Barrett doesn't condone overt demonstration and you look determinedly overt."

"Okay, so I'm overt!"

"Meet me when the moon rises back of the corral tonight and let us be real overt—but right now let this little punk have a chance to reassemble his dignity. It isn't his knee that hurts. He's just proud. He's limping just in case he cries. Then he'll have something reasonably respectable to tie his tears on. Come on now—we'll take an intense interest in these flower beds. Hook onto a daisy or two like a good girl." Docilely I started picking posies.

"But, Joe," I protested, "he feels abandoned." I saw him standing alone, biting his fingernails. I wasn't supposed to let him do that.

"Yep—he *is* abandoned, you know, as certainly as if he'd

just been deposited in a basket on a strange doorstep. This is a haven for abandoned waifs, kiddo."

"Oh, Joe," Warren said. "Don't give us another of your lectures. Sure the kids get in the home-folks' hair, but the bulk of our students at The Oaks are here because of the superior educational facilities we offer. After all, Hargrave, you've got to admit that this is a good school."

"Oh, sure, it's okay, but it could be better and it's not as good as even a Grade B home. Anyway, remember, Fluff, and you, Warren, 'superior educational facilities' is a benign false face that conceals many motivations and is so effective it has anesthetized the wearer into forgetting the true nature of his own damn ugly mug behind the mask. It's all fine for the older boys—I approve when they're over twelve. But these little guys—they're snatched from the good-night kiss and made into manly little handshakers before their time."

"Well, Barrett says, and I think he's right," Warren argued, "that in England children are regularly sent to boarding school at the age of eight. The results are splendidly educated and highly independent individuals."

"Oh poof—a pox on Barrett! I'd like to kick him in his London derrière. Jeffrey's regaining consciousness now. I'll take him over. You two go back to the tea guzzlers. Warren, see that our ingénue here meets Mrs. Byrne-Masterson while she's still Mrs. Byrne-Masterson. She's a chameleon and changes personalities with husbands and right now she's sort of neutral. Next time she shows up she'll probably be a hearty sportswoman—or maybe a viola player, according to what prey she bags. I, for one, wish she'd snag a child psychologist just long enough to rear Kevin."

"Hey, Carruthers!" Joe walked over toward the boy who had finally managed to turn a fairly composed face toward us. "I've just discovered it's time to feed my dogs. Some of the boys usually help me. Do you happen to be free now?

Maybe you'd lend me a hand. There are three of them, and I can't manage three pans."

"Oh yes, sir—yes, I do happen to be free now, and I'd sure be glad to help you." They walked off toward the kitchen in a rumble of dog talk. I was consoled to note that Jeffrey had lost his limp.

"He's fed those three dogs of his four times already this afternoon." Warren shook his head and tapped his temple with his first finger. "But I must say it's sound therapy. He always starves them for a day before school opens to keep them eager, and then gives them just enough at each feeding to tantalize them. Nothing seems to make a boy feel so much at home as being on good terms with the dogs."

"And on good terms with Joe, maybe," I offered, as my marveling eye followed the tall, "unpleasant creature" and the rapt little boy.

"Dear Gigi," I wrote a quick one that night. "I'm afraid I like the boys *very much* indeed—and you'd be surprised what an age range that covers. . . ."

CHAPTER SIX

Boy Crazy

My LETTER to Gigi was prophetic. My fears that I liked the boys very much indeed were justified. I don't know exactly when I succumbed completely to the spell of my charges and became a full-fledged victim. I suppose actually it was love at first sight.

I discovered, however, that there are certain advantages in having the objects of a lady's love range in age from eight to thirteen. Nobody raises an eyebrow and dubs you fickle just because you're mad about thirty or forty at the same time. And, even though the entire forty may be all-gone guys over you, you still are not accused of "leading them on."

Some of the boys were perhaps slightly more attractive to me than others, but I was far from discriminating. On a different level, I suspect, I was somewhat like a friend of mine. I inquired once about her enthusiasm for a current beau. "What's so wonderful about *him?*"

"He's a man," she said.

Joe diagnosed me. "Let us face it, Flower Face," he said. "You're not only inconsistent—you hated schoolteaching and everything that went with it not six weeks ago—but now you're the noisiest trumpet on the band wagon. You're just plain boy crazy."

56

"All right," I admitted, "so I'm boy crazy, but at my age it's a becoming womanly virtue, you know, and they call it maternalism."

"How's about you sort of slipping me in unobtrusively among the rest of the rogues?"

"Hum—?" I squinted my eyes at him. "No, Mr. Hargrave, your willingness is laudable, but I don't think you'll do. You're too old for me. You'll never see ten again."

"But, if you're real sharp, you'll realize that, in one respect at least, I'm superior to the rest of these fluff faces of yours."

"Name your superior trait."

"Well—I'm through puberty."

"But, my dear—so many achieve *that*. Even Barrett. I'll string along with Pete Matthews with his dark, good looks, and Bobby Lennox with his irresistible blond charm. *All* the Acorns send me. They look like a covey of cherubs."

"They do, for a fact," agreed Joe. "But every single one of them secretly thinks he's a Boris Karloff. They prefer frightening-type men. They will, of course, tolerate two-gun handsome guys like Buck Rogers, the Lone Ranger, and *me*, but generally speaking, they fancy themselves as Jack the Ripper."

"And they are so witty—my Acorns—dazzlingly so. Just say 'Sanka,' and in a flash, they all yell in chorus, 'You're welcome.' And then we all laugh like crazy. There's never a dull moment. You can see why you don't stand up against the competition of such beauty and brilliance."

There was no doubt of it, whatever slight preferences I had among the boys were pretty much on the basis of age. The eights and nines made more real emotional impact on me than any of the others. This may have been partly proximity, for these were, of course, the boys with whom I spent most of my time.

But also, to be needed, so I am told, is a strong girder in the

structure of love. My Acorns needed me. It was wonderful
for the Pines to have Joe for a friend, but they did not need
him in the same way. Twelve- and thirteen-year-old boys are
ready to go off to boarding school. It may even be the best
place in the world for them. But eight- and nine-year-old boys
aren't ready for boarding school. Home is the best place in the
world for them. That sounds categorical, and it is. It's just
as uncontroversial as "a rose is a rose is a rose. . . ."

All the Acorns were installed in Kirkland Hall under my
supervision. I took Joe's advice and tore up Dr. Barrett's
three-by-five filing cards with their apocryphal thumbnail
sketches. Joe was right, even a lyric poet with a psychiatrist's
degree could not properly have recorded the essence of the
Acorns. I learned about the boys by living with them. I not
only got them up in the morning—or more honestly, they
got me up—and heckled them into brushing their teeth, I
also taught them most of the day. Then I dawdled the evening
hours away with them until bedtime and tooth-brush-heckling
time again. And many were the nocturnal hours I spent with
them. For little boys at school, as at home, get stomach-aches,
croup, nightmares, fall out of bed occasionally, and sometimes
get up and roam around just for the pure hell of it.

But little boys at school have one nocturnal problem not
common to boys under the parental roof. This problem was
the first traumatic challenge I experienced as a boarding-
school teacher. They sometimes get homesick.

They themselves are likely to misdiagnose this malady as
stomach-ache, sore knee, earache, toothache, poison ivy, or,
those willing to skirt that close to the truth, may even say they
are crying because someone was mean to them. *Never* did I
hear a little boy say simply and forthrightly, "I'm homesick,"
or "I want my mother."

"My stomach aches" was the favorite fraud, but given in
good faith. They *thought* they had stomach-aches. They often

did. That's what psychiatrists call psychosomatic disorders. Not being a psychiatrist, however, it took me a while to learn to distinguish between Type I and Type II stomach-aches.

I discovered in time, of course, that the Type II malaise is, for the most part, a seasonal disease. It is usually epidemic following summer vacation and "new" boys are likely to be hardest hit, having built up no immunity to the disease. It frequently breaks out in mild form after Thanksgiving and Christmas holidays. I found that tears are rarely symptomatic of anything except the Type II virus. Eating not wisely but too well, or nipping a few too many chocolate sodas on a wild Saturday afternoon on the town might very well make a nine-year-old throw up but it rarely made him cry. Eventually, I could just sniff the air and diagnose intuitively.

Type I stomach-aches I treated on the spot with a hot-water bottle, a swig of Kaopectate or Milk of Magnesia, a hand on the brow while the basin was utilized, a few affectionate pats, and my best bedside manner until sleep overtook the sufferer.

The treatment of Type II stomach-aches, on the other hand, was more complex. Such cases were removed from bed, put into their slippers and robes, and taken to my living room, where they were allowed to sit or lie, as the spirit moved them, on my sofa in front of my fire. Here the prescription was not Milk of Magnesia but hot chocolate made on my electric plate.

Of course, there was no magic maternal inner prompting that diagnosed my cases for me. In fact, it took me a long time to learn the subtle distinction between Type I and Type II. Joe served as consultant on my first few baffling patients.

Bobby Lennox was in for treatment one night. A man and a woman alone in front of a fire 'way late at night—it was *already* ten-thirty!—are likely to warm up to each other and indulge themselves in strangely beautiful and memorable

communication. My Type II stomach-ache cases and I were
no exception. Between sniffles and the muffling caused by
a fist being rubbed under his nose, Bobby apprised me of the
state of his stomach.

"I sure do (sniff) have a—a (sniff) awful stom–m–m–mach-
ache," he sobbed.

"I know," I agreed sympathetically, and automatically
handed him a Kleenex. Sick or well, Bobby never carried a
pocket handkerchief. "It's a shame, but I'm not giving you
Milk of Magnesia because I think it's muscular. I watched
you playing football today and I swear I never in my life saw
a boy run so fast. Goodness! I was proud of you, but when
you were charging with the ball, you twisted around *so*
adroitly, I just bet you strained a muscle. Hot drinks are good
for that sort of thing."

"Did you think I ran fast?"

"Oh, I certainly did!"

"I can run fas–faster (sniff—mild type) than that *even*."

"Really! Oh, honestly you *amaze* me, Bobby. I feel so lucky
to have you for one of my students. It makes me terribly
proud."

To be amazed and proud of a homesick boy and to be terribly lucky to have him for a student is about the best line
a teacher can string. My sentiment was real enough, but synthetic compared to what he needed to hear—that someone
was pleased and proud and terribly lucky to have him for her
own little boy. But it's like treatment of the common cold.
If there isn't any aureomycin available, it's dopey not at least
to *try* a dose of aspirin tablets.

Even if Bobby had been at home—where he obviously
wanted to be—there was no one there particularly pleased to
have him for a son. Bobby's mother and father were about to
get a divorce—and each one apparently had offered to make
the "great sacrifice" to the other and relinquish the custody

of Bobby. According to Joe, to whom Mrs. Lennox always unloaded "what she suffered," the only thing that had kept them together the last year had been the fact that this problem could not be resolved. Mrs. Lennox kept insisting she wouldn't deprive Mr. Lennox of Bobby and Mr. Lennox, just as vehemently, insisted he wouldn't take the boy away from his mother. They were so sacrificial and fair-minded with each other on the issue that they were at an unfortunate stalemate.

Bobby ran his fist under his nose again. "You sure do make good chocolate." He took a noisy swig. "Better'n my mother makes, I betcha."

He suddenly announced, with a certain vindictiveness that when he grew up he thought he'd be a schoolmaster. "And I'll marry a lady teacher like you, too, and then we'll live in the school, and you know what?"

"What?" I asked.

"Well, then if we had some kids, they could live with us. They could go to school right at home. I just betcha that kids whose fathers teach school live with their folks *all* the time. Then me and my wife would go and talk to our own children special every single night."

"But you'd like all the other children in the school very much, too, wouldn't you?"

"No. They wouldn't be our children."

"I think you would. You couldn't help it. I couldn't help liking you, for instance, Bobby. As a matter of fact, I love all the boys in this school."

"Yeh?—Pete and Larry and Kevin and all them? You love me, *too*, huh?"

"Oh—very much."

He paused to think over my tender declaration.

"You're okay, too," he wooed back. He yawned. He crawled a little closer to me on the couch and leaned his head back against my shoulder. I put my arm around him. He sighed, wiggled himself into comfort, and yawned again—more contentedly than sleepily.

Dr. Barrett was of the opinion that "All the support necessary for a schoolboy can be given without physical demonstration. No overt gestures of affection, please." Being of a suspicious nature, he explained this carefully to me immediately after my arrival at The Oaks. At the time it didn't occur to me that I had suppressed urges to run around kissing grubby little boys—but I certainly underestimated my own weaknesses! I succumbed to them, too, occasionally. There were times, in fact, when a quick clandestine kiss on a forehead or a subversive hug, delivered in strictest privacy, seemed the only possible course for me to take. Moreover, the victims, I thoroughly believe, appreciated my dereliction—for all their brusque acceptance. Certainly Bobby relaxed in my arms and his brave, restrained sniffles subsided completely.

He paused a moment as if seeking just the right words. Then with a certain charming reticence he made his passionate avowal. "Us kids are glad you're here even though you're a dame. We think you're quite sharp. Mr. Hargrave says you're pretty, too." He gave me a skeptical and appraising scrutiny. "You do look okay."

One nice thing about trusting your love to an eight-year-old, you can always be sure that no matter what charming extravagances he whispers in your ear, he doesn't say it to *all* the girls.

"My mother is sure sharp, too—real pretty. She and my dad are going to get a divorce and both of them want me. They can't decide who's going to have me, though."

"I should think it would be very hard for either one to give you up, Bobby. Which do you think you'd rather be with?"

"Oh—I don't know. I guess both of them would miss me terribly." Since Bobby hit the home doorstep only about one

week end in two months, what with school in winter and
camp in summer, I felt that probably both of the Lennoxes
were gently broken in to face their loss. "You know what—
I'll tell you something." Bobby paused a moment as if appraising me as proper confidante. "I might really be adopted."

"Oh?"

"Yep—quite often I figure I am. Of course, my parents
like me so much they wouldn't ever tell me about being
adopted. But I sure don't look like them and I can't read good
or anything and they're both real smart. My father said when
he was big as I am, he could spell practically any old word that
ever was invented."

"Well—when I was your age, I couldn't spell." I didn't go
on and admit my current handicap in that area.

"One day I thought I saw my real mother," Bobby said
dreamily.

"Where did you see her?" I prodded gently.

"In Los Angeles—at Bullocks-Wilshire. My mother was
trying on dresses and stuff and she said how's about me stop
wiggling and get the hell out of there and walk around by
myself till she got done and meet her in the parking lot. It
was that time I saw her."

"What made you think the woman was your mother?"

"Well—she wasn't, I guess. Several other times I thought
I saw my real mother, too, but it was like then. This woman
was just walking along, see, with two other boys and I figured
they might be my long-lost brothers. When I came along, she
looked at me sort of like she knew me."

"Did she speak to you?"

"Well, see—I said, 'Hello,' and I just stood there to see if
she recognized me. She said, 'Well—hello there,' like she was
pleased—real pleased. But then she went right on and one
of the boys said, 'Who's that kid, Mom?' and I heard her say,
'How should I know, Jerry?' "

He wiggled around a little. "You haven't got any kids, have you?"

"No but I wish I did. I'd love to have a boy just like you."

"I suppose you'd remember if you ever did have a boy that got lost or kidnaped or something?"

"Yes, I think I'd remember."

"Yep, I guess you would. Besides, I'm *not* adopted really. I even asked my mother once and she said, 'I'll say you're not adopted and the stork didn't bring you either, that's for sure.' She looked real mad—I guess it hurt her feelings, me thinking I wasn't her own boy—like that, see?"

What was it Barrett had put on this little boy's three-by-five card? "Can't read well or spell (correct)." I kissed him lightly behind his left ear. The technique was not recommended in any of the Education texts I'd flipped through, but I had a feeling it might be a specific for reading disability.

"Know any good jokes?" he asked me then. The Type II stomach-ache palliative was working. He was about ready for bed now. I would have told him a joke if I could have thought of one, but the wit was drained out of me.

"Can't remember any at the moment, but I tell you what— I'll think up a good one before English class first hour tomorrow. How's about hitting the hay, fellow?"

Filtering his speech through a wide yawn, he said, "But I'm not a *bit* sleepy."

CHAPTER SEVEN

Sons in Their Courses

W<small>HAT</small> with practicing psychosomatic medicine, sewing on buttons, pulling out loose teeth, acting as impresario for bathing and dressing routines, giving ethical and moral instruction, refereeing fist fights, etc., it is small wonder that at times I tended to forget that I was hired basically as a classroom teacher. My students were supposed to learn reading and spelling from me, plus a few facts like the name of the fourteenth president of the United States and the agricultural products of Brazil, so they'd have something to forget and learn over when they got to high school.

In advance contemplation, this facet of my job had caused me no anxiety whatsoever. It didn't occur to me that there was anything really complicated about teaching eight- and nine-year-old boys. To deliver a neat package of alegebra or Latin might present a challenge, but I certainly had no qualms about stacking my bachelor-of-arts degree against the curriculum of third- and fourth-grade elementary school.

"Turn to page seven of *Billy and Betty Visit the Circus* and we'll take turns reading aloud." That was my idea of third-grade teaching.

My disenchantment was not long in coming. Curriculum I could cope with, but I hadn't taken into account curiosity.

65

The questions that flow out of the mouths of normal eight-
and nine-year-olds would stretch the mind of Einstein.

"What do I do when they ask me perfectly fiendish questions?" I demanded of Joe. "Do I admit I don't know? They
expect me to be able to spell every word in *Webster's Un-
abridged Dictionary*, and know how many teeth a frog has,
and how far it is to the nearest star and whether men on Mars
speak English, and who invented roller skates."

"Introduce them to the dictionary and the encyclopedia,"
Joe advised. "Every time you can't answer a question or spell
a word, just say that this is a fine opportunity for them to
learn to do their own research. Send them off to the library
with a pencil and paper to look up 'frog' or how to spell
'onomatopoeia.' If every one of them conveniently pops you
a poser at the same time, you can get rid of the whole mess
of them and read a novel."

This proved a very useful device, but I never had a chance
to read a novel. For one thing, the device was no help with
Bobby Lennox, who, alas, couldn't read—and it was useless
with Homer, who knew everything and tantalized me by
giving information rather than asking for it.

Even Joe couldn't solve Bobby for me. Bobby was a non-
reader. There are a variety of reasons, I suppose, for a child's
being unable to read. "He's left-eyed," or "He's left-handed,"
are nice, simple explanations. Bobby's father explained it
even more simply. "That kid just won't apply himself. Won't
put his mind to things—or maybe he's just plain dumb."

Bobby wasn't dumb, and with a frantic eagerness he put
his mind to things. He picked up a third-grade reader as if
it were a bomb about to detonate. He looked at the print and
his eyes became glazed with fright, and his hand shook when
he wet his finger to turn the pages. When called upon to
read, he looked quickly at the pictures illustrating the text
for a clue and then attempted to guess what might be writ-

ten about them. His guesses revealed little of the author's intentions in most instances, but they were probably very revealing of Bobby's problems.

I remember one day he interpreted a picture of a small boy crying by "reading": "Billy is crying because he is lost and cannot find his mother or his father." Actually, Billy was crying because he had skinned his knee.

Teaching Bobby was no cinch for an amateur. I read everything I could put my hands on regarding reading disabilities. Dr. Fernald of the University of California suggested the kinesthetic approach to reading—the tracing with the fingers of words, written in large script on poster-size paper. Miraculously, so it seemed to me, this worked with Bobby. Forced to feel the letters with his fingers, he finally became friendly enough with words to look at them with his eyes.

I found myself giving Bobby two individual tutoring hours out of my precious time each day, but it was worth it. His joy when he was able slowly but accurately to read a sentence in class was matched only by my rejoicing and that of his classmates! The boys all liked Bobby and they suffered almost as much acute agony over his scholastic failure as he did.

Not to call on Bobby in class would have been too obvious in motivation. His embarrassment over special privilege would have been greater than his embarrassment over blundering recitations. Still, I felt obliged to save him, and also save myself and his friends from our painful empathy. So— carefully I contrived a method to assure him success.

Every day or so I called on the boys in the order of their seating, asking each one to read a question and answer it. Only naïve teachers with holes in their heads slip into this pedagogical pitfall. Each pupil, of course, quickly counts down to the sentence that is to be his chore and is fully prepared for a sharp reply. My little boys always eyed each other roguishly whenever I announced this procedure. One day I even caught

Peter tapping his forehead with his finger, with accompany-
ing facial grimaces implying to his friend, Jamie, that I was
a lame-brain. They thought they were outwitting me smartly
and that it had never occurred to me that they would antici-
pate their sentences long before being called upon.

Bobby, like the others, counted down to his question and
laboriously sounded out the words over and over under his
breath. Then with the pride of a general announcing a victory against overwhelming odds, he read his assignment when
called upon.

Before very long, the boys quit pitying Bobby, and Bobby
quit having "stomach-aches." None of them ever noticed that
Bobby was always spared when recitations were in random
order. By the end of the year, Bobby was without doubt the
worst reader in the third grade. But that was his greatest
triumph, for to be judged the worst reader, he at least had
to read.

I suppose the only thing that is harder on a teacher than
a very dull or blocked student is an excessively brilliant one.
After all, a dullard is at least reassuring in definition of roles.
There's no question of who's teacher and who's pupil. Being
Educatress to a little boy like Homer William Curtis (named
for the Epic Poet and the Bard of Avon) inflicted on me a
frightening inferiority complex. With Homer, I felt reluctant
to speak with authority on anything more controversial than
how to spell "cat."

Homer had on tap an incredible collection of miscellaneous
and usually deadly accurate facts. Dan Golenpaugh and
Clifton Fadiman would have loved Homer.

He was a day boy from a small ranch near the school. This
at least was cause for rejoicing. Contriving dinner conversation for Homer would have finished me. His father was a
New England college professor who was spending a year in
the Southwest fighting through asthma and the writing of a

book on the "Major Prophets of the Nineteenth Century."
If anyone a hundred years from now writes a similar treatise
on "The Major Prophets of the Twentieth Century," I'll be
one mighty surprised angel if Homer Curtis's name doesn't
lead all the rest.

Homer was nine and so fell into my grade-three and four
classes, called, for purpose of stylish confusion, "Forms I and
II." According to the Stanford Achievement Test, Homer
should have been slugging it out in high school and on the
Binet-Simon Scale his I.Q. touched 178, without any notice-
able strain. His parents felt that Homer would be better off
socially, however, if he weren't pushed beyond his own age
group. His own age group, alas, would have been considerably
better off socially if Homer had been pushed—even shoved!

I had Homer in English, History, and Arts and Crafts.
Only in the latter was I in the driver's seat. Homer could
handle a water-color brush or a wad of clay about as grace-
fully as a walrus could handle a ball-point pen. Even so,
the arts-and-crafts hour twice a week was hardly sufficient to
build up my ego after having it deflated twice a day in English and History.

Homer was always polite. He invariably asked for permission before speaking his mind.

He had me quietly on the defensive and he had every boy
in the class noisily so.

We'd read something out of a supposedly sound fourth-
grade history textbook, and Homer would wave his hand
frantically in the air.

Eventually, I'd feel obliged to acknowledge him. After all,
there was always the possibility he wanted to tell me his ap-
pendix had just burst.

"Would you care to hear what *actually* happened?"

"Why, yes, Homer," I'd lie for the sake of free speech. I had
little enthusiasm for what actually happened.

Getting the real low-down on the heroes of history from Homer usually proved a little tiresome and often very disillusioning.

For instance, Homer had some admiration for "The Father of Our Country," but he certainly had no father fixation about him—that was for sure. He was unwilling to let anyone entertain any illusions about George. Homer wouldn't even tolerate our decorating the classroom windows with cutouts of hatchets on Washington's birthday.

"After all," he said, "it has in no way been established that Washington ever cut down a cherry tree. As for his never telling a lie, our own logic prevents us from accepting that myth."

The rest of the boys just sat and glared darkly at Homer and the atmosphere throbbed with antipathy. Little boys are very suspicious of glib vocabulary in their contemporaries.

"Lookit!" Peter Matthews spoke up. "Let's make hatchets anyway. You can't prove he didn't *own* a hatchet, can you, Homer?"

"No," admitted Homer. "He may very well have owned a hatchet. That's possible. But—may I point out that Washington was a gentleman? He probably never used a hatchet in his life. He had servants who undoubtedly did all menial work for him."

"Baloney!" yelled Peter.

"Baloney!" echoed Bobby Lennox.

"Baloney!" came a chorus.

"Keep your baloney in your lunch baskets, boys," I said. The Acorns liked that type of humor. It was what Joe and I always called being "A-corny." Anyway, it worked much better than unvarnished correction.

"What I say is still 'irrefutional,'" said Homer. Only the fact that Homer very occasionally misconstructed a word sustained me and kept me from swapping desks with him.

"Accepted as pure legend," I said, "the story of the cherry

tree is picturesque and hatchets have become a symbol of Washington's birthday. I see no harm at all, Homer, in our cutting out a few to decorate our windows."

"Bourgeois," muttered Homer—which was a word his father threw around rather aimlessly, too.

Of course, the hatchets created a minor ripple compared to Homer's dramatic and somewhat mystifying revelations about Abraham Lincoln's mother.

"It is a very interesting fact," Homer began one day when we were reading about Honest Abe. Frankly, I usually found Homer's facts somewhat less than fascinating. "It is interesting," he said, "that Abraham Lincoln's mother, Nancy Hanks, was illegitimate."

"There is some reason, perhaps, to believe that Nancy Hanks may have been illegitimate," I said warily.

I took a quick look at my watch. It was certainly leaning on Fate, but I was hoping the bell was about to ring. Barrett had told us that Sex Education was the responsibility of parents. If any questions pertaining to this "delicate subject" came up, they were to be referred to him personally. We were certainly skirting the edges of the delicate subject.

"What's it mean?" demanded Peter.

" 'Illegitimate' merely means that she was born out of wedlock." I affected a cheerful tone of voice hoping I could delay and mystify them with a new word.

"Wedlock?" asked Bobby. "What's wedlock?"

"Can you explain 'wedlock' Homer?" Any minute now the bell should ring. Ring out, wild bell—let her rip!

"Certainly," said Homer. "Wedlock—often called 'holy wedlock'—is the marriage of a man and woman by church ceremony. Then children born of that union are legitimate. Otherwise they're illegitimate or bastards."

"Oh! What you said, Homer Curtis! That's a very bad word, isn't it?" demanded Jeffrey Carruthers.

"No," I said, "the word 'bastard' in itself isn't bad. It is just that it has been given a rather unpleasant connotation. It has frequently been misused to imply deficiency in character."

"Huh—" sneered Jeffrey. "I'm not 'gitimate' myself then. My mother and father got married by the Justice of the Peace in New Jersey one Saturday night after a dance when no churches were open or anything. They weren't even in a church. And I'm not a bastard, so there!"

"Is Jeffrey a bastard?" demanded Kevin Clark, obviously awed.

"No, certainly not. Jeffrey is not a bastard," I said cheerfully. "He's legitimate. Homer did not define 'wedlock' quite properly." Everyone looked exceedingly pleased at this.

"Homer failed to explain that wedlock is the state of marriage, whether performed in civil ceremony or in church ceremony."

"Yah—see, Smarty!" sneered Peter Matthews.

By adroit maneuvering I had been able to achieve a momentary victory over Homer. Oh dear—before Homer attacked me with another uncomfortable fact—why, oh why, didn't that damned bell ring? It did.

CHAPTER EIGHT

Feathered and Other Friends

Even today, after a long, arduous indoctrination, I am certainly no Lady Hiawatha. I don't want to be a sister or anything else to the Wild Goose. I don't want to cozy up to any feathered friends. I like birds—but birds, in my opinion, are strictly for the birds. The same goes for beasts. To each his own, I always say.

Of course, just drop a broken-winged nestling in my lap and I'll make an exception in his case—or an orphaned bunny rabbit. But I simply won't go out of my way to establish intimacy with animals.

My dog, who happens to be lying on my feet at the moment, just woke up to attack a flea. He's a self-made dog who supported himself for years as a migrant before I met him. Now that I think about it, I guess I did pick *him* up in a bar. And the cat asleep on my desk—actually, he *was* someone I met in an alley. He gave me a fairly convincing hard-luck story about the mice shortage and his extreme youth, and I brought him home to put him up for a few nights. He's been here *seven* years now! Of course, dogs and cats are different—or are they?

Oh, let's face it—when I taught school, I not only learned to love little boys, I learned to love their livestock—most of

73

it anyway. I never did get around to having cozy consortium with any of the snakes. Little boys attract animals—or vice versa—like a magnet attracts steel shavings. A boy and a dog, for instance, seem to me to be as essential to each other as Gilbert and Sullivan or Rodgers and Hart or beer and pretzels.

But little boys don't stop at basic essentials. What every little boy in this country needs is a good five-cent dog, I'll grant that. But I never knew a boy who would settle for just a dog. My little boys introduced me to the charms of baby birds, bunnies, bassarisks, skunks, coyotes, cats, dogs, mice, et cetera ad infinitum—and *snakes.*

The first time I saw a snake crawl out of a little boy's pocket, slither down his leg, and make a deliberate tour of my classroom, I don't mind admitting I was ruffled.

"I think I see a snake," I said uneasily.

"Oh! that's mine!" yelled Peter. "That's Marmalade. Where'd he come from? I been looking for him."

"I thought he came out of Jamie Travers's pocket—but I could be wrong," I said. "I *hoped* I was wrong at the time I *thought* I saw him come out of Jamie Travers's pocket."

"So—you're the one who hid my snake, huh, Jamie?" Peter obviously felt some very strong emotion about this creature but it was a very different emotion from my own. He jumped up and ran over and gathered up tenderly every repulsive inch of the reptile. Jamie jumped up, too.

"Now, you lookit!" yelled Jamie. "You gave me Marmalade, Peter Matthews, so there. We swapped fair and square. You took that white mouse of mine—Cordelia—in exchange. You know you did."

"Yah—but you're a cheater, so there," said Peter. "You said Cordelia was fat because she was going to have babies, and I was going to sell the babies and make some money." This ambition of Peter's seemed a little superfluous, since he supposedly already had a six-million-dollar trust fund cooling in the vault until he was twenty-one.

"Well—" Jamie defended himself. "I *said* I didn't *know* for *sure* about the babies. It was Homer said she was pregnant."

"I did not!" Now Homer was in it. "I never once actually said she was pregnant. I *said* that Cordelia *looked* as if she were gestating."

"Phooie on it, Homer!" Peter simply couldn't tolerate Homer's vocabulary. "Mr. Carson, he says *that* mouse isn't even a lady mouse. She's a man—and can't have babies even. I named her over. Her name's George now—and I want my snake back because that's fair, isn't it, sir?" It was not unusual for the boys to call me "sir." This was established habit, as well as rule, in addressing the masters, and they kept forgetting my unique status.

To sit in judgment on the problem at hand was something for which I was ill prepared. I had seen Cordelia-George— an unpleasant-looking white mouse, somewhat on the tubby side. I had seen a lot of white mice, as a matter of fact. Every boy who could get his hands on the capital had bought one three weeks before. A man in Flagstaff who was breeding them to sell to the college biochemistry laboratory had got a little overstocked and knew a good market when he saw one. Fortunately, some of the boys hadn't been able to raise the twenty-five cents. Anyway—although I had been introduced to numerous mice and even knew Cordelia-George well enough to recognize her if she got loose in my room, I didn't know whether this unpleasant, fat, nonpregnant mouse, sex male, was a fair trade for this unpleasant, thin snake, sex unknown. What they teach you in college is pretty esoteric when it comes to life situations. Even Solomon would have felt challenged, I imagine.

"Right now," I said, "I suggest that Marmalade be taken

away and put in his—or her—cage. The case will come up for
review at recess. This snake is not a registered member of
my Form I English class, and I don't think the use of the
comma will interest him in the least. Take him out, Peter—
you may go too, Jamie."

They walked out together, still arguing. They put Marmalade into a ventilated carton in the patio. Apparently, the
carton was too well ventilated, however. At recess, anyway,
it was discovered and announced in wild shouts that Marmalade had taken a powder.

This was a relief to me. I had gotten over my bigotry about
mice, and had even learned to accept them socially. "After all,
they're animals, same as anyone else," Peter had explained
to me during my brief span of intolerance. However, the Eve
in me balked—I recognized my basic feminine distrust of
snakes. I was unwilling to admit that *they* were animals the
same as anyone else. I frankly hated them—and they haven't
grown on me over the years.

Marmalade, gone, presented another judicial problem. To
whom did the surviving piece of property belong? Who was
the legal owner of Cordelia-George? Jamie, with little grace,
mumbling unpleasant words under his breath—"Cheater!
Sneak! Thief!"—finally yielded him to Peter. Peter didn't
actually want him, since George was not about to become a
mother. But it was a matter of honor with him to claim his
rights. After all, a mouse in the hand is worth a snake in the
grass any day.

But if the snake *were* in the grass, the boys were going to
find him. At recess, all the Acorns threw themselves, with
noble dedication, into a Marmalade man hunt. Marmalade
outwitted them, however. So far as I know, he is still a fugi-
tive. However, they did find seven other snakes—most of
them much bigger and more repulsive than Marmalade.

Fortunately, they even uncovered a desert diamondback

rattlesnake. I say "fortunately," not from fiendishness, but because the diamondback, who rattled just in time to dissuade Jeffy Carruthers from picking him up, pointed out the perils of reptile collecting. Dr. Barrett laid down an excellent protective law. Only Peter and Jamie among the first formers were to be permitted to collect snakes. Both had studied all the pictures and most of the text in Ditmars' reptile book and they were regarded as reliable enough not to pause to engage in any small talk with rattlers—or that much rarer and more insidious menace in Arizona, the coral snake.

So all the seven snakes were installed in cartons in Peter's room, which was somewhat more commodious than Jamie's. He and Jamie cared for the snakes, and all the other boys in my hall were sort of common stockholders in the venture.

In passing, I might mention that incarcerated snakes smell.

I suppose I communicated my "disinterest" in snakes too vehemently—which was a great mistake. A little boy may be filled to the brim with the milk of human kindness, but what rises to the top isn't necessarily cream. With little boys, even of noblest character, it is always open season on lady snake-haters.

The Acorns realized, I am sure, that my wariness was such that I'd rather have curled up in a lion's den, complete with toothy lions, than pick up a snake.

So—one night. I was entertaining the faculty at afterdinner coffee in my sitting room. The little boys were dashing up and down the corridor outside, as usual. They were holding whispered consultations—pungent with giggles. One of my ears was always tuned in on corridor activities—the other I tuned in on my adult companions.

Luckily, Bobby always whispered in high voice. He was the Judas in the plotted betrayal. "She just *hates* them, see—" he whispered. "She hates them. Let's take the biggest one,

Damrosch, and give him to her as a present and see if she screams." Some fun!

Damrosch was named for Walter Damrosch, the admirable gentleman who conducted the radio Junior Standard Symphony to which the boys listened weekly. They didn't regard Damrosch as a snake. In fact, they loved him dearly since by choosing to listen to his program they were excused from Math class. The name was selected merely because they could then, with impunity, call their dear pet "Dam" for short. If they were reproved, they could always insist that "Dam" was not a bad word but an innocent snake's name. The Acorns thought this was wondrously wicked and riotously humorous.

So I heard more whispers, and shortly there was a knock at my open door. Peter and Jamie stood there holding up between them four feet of what *silly* people call a "harmless gopher snake."

"We decided to give you one of our snakes," said Peter in a benign manner that wouldn't have fooled a foggy-headed half-wit. "Dam's our biggest and best one, so we picked him."

"Yeh," agreed dear little Jamie—and butter wouldn't have melted in his mouth. "We want you to have our *very* best snake."

This is my darkest hour, I thought. My time of trial by fire was upon me. What I did now would make or break my tomorrows. All the masters were gazing upon me with almost as much impish interest as Jamie and Peter. In a situation like this, every man has cement in his glove, that's for sure.

I knew that I had to pay the price.

"Why—what a generous thought," I said. "It's just the nicest thing anyone ever did for me. Thank you so much."

I took delivery. I reached out for Damrosch. Sobered, the boys handed him to me. Damrosch promptly curled himself cozily around my arm. I strode back to my chair—and they say it's psychologically rugged to walk to the guillotine! I sat down and encouraged Damrosch to give me back my arm. I then laid him on my lap—although he wouldn't relax, and hung over a little on both sides, so that he could remind my legs, too, that he was there. I went on drinking my coffee, pausing only occasionally to caress Damrosch with my hand and murmur sweet nothings to him—"Damn, *Damn*, Damn," was the way I put it up to him.

Peter and Jamie by this time were backed up by a covey of definitely deflated Acorns. They looked upon me, it is true, with awe, wonder, and perhaps a touch of admiration, but diluted considerably by their obvious disappointment.

Damrosch started to crawl down my leg. I pulled him back forcefully and said a few firm but tender words to him. It was not fun.

Finally the boys retreated. "Yeeps—she likes snakes," I heard Peter say. "She *loves* them. Honestly, Bobby, you make me plenty mad. Dam was our best snake, too—now we'll *never* get him back. Whatever made you think she'd scream?"

"I don't know," apologized Bobby. "I'm sure sorry."

I allowed Damrosch to roam about my room all evening. When it was bedtime for the boys, I went down the hall as usual to tell them "good night." I took Dam with me. He pulled that unpleasant trick of his, and wound himself around my arm. I mentioned his charms to every boy.

When I got to Peter's room, I said, "Peter this is the nicest snake I ever knew." (This wasn't much of a lie. I hadn't known many snakes, and the difference between the nicest and the nastiest was half a hairsbreadth.)

"Yeh—he's okay, I guess," agreed Peter with feigned in- difference.

"This is awfully disappointing," I told Peter, "and I do hope you won't be insulted, but you know Dr. Barrett's rule. All snakes are supposed to be in cages, and I have no place to keep Damrosch. Frankly, I don't know what to do with him."

"Well—you know what," said Peter. "I could keep him here in his regular cage, sort of."

"Oh, would you?"

"Sure, I don't mind a bit."

"Well—thank you, Peter. That solves everything. Here he is." I handed him over.

Peter took him in his arms. "Well, you old Dammy," he cooed at him tenderly. "I'll put you to bed now, that's just what I'll do."

"Good night, dear," I said. I went back to my room to have my postponed nervous breakdown.

"Hey, guys!" Peter yelled down the hall. "Hey, guys! Everything's swell!"

You can say that again, Pete, I thought to myself.

From then on, they *heartlessly* deprived me of all sociability with their reptiles. They were afraid I'd get too attached to them. Certainly nobody ever offered me a snake again. They *knew* I'd grab it.

CHAPTER NINE

Not Cheaper by the Dozen

THE day after school reconvened following Thanksgiving holidays, Joe stopped me on my way to breakfast. "What's wrong with your weepers, Wonderful?" I was easy to stop since I had about as much momentum as a snail that had been overindulging in barbiturates.

"Don't speak to me or I'll scream!" I answered.

"Have you been lying awake all night with the hot blood pounding in your veins, thinking of me? You look like a part-time witch, if you'll pardon the expression. You mustn't do this sort of thing to yourself. Just yell out the window when you get in such a mood and I'll come right over."

"Listen, you two-bit bench warmer," I said, "I've been up half the night, and not thinking of you, that's for sure!"

"What are you venting your spleen about? So you have bags under your eyes. I don't mind. You know I don't care how you look. You're the only woman around here, and frankly, there's something about you that appeals to me. You bring out the stark heterosexual in me."

"So—I have bags under my eyes! Thank you so much— and do you know why I have them?"

"No, but I'll listen—although I can't think of a single fascinating place to get bags under the eyes within two hundred miles of here."

It had been a *night!* It wasn't that anything unusual happened. It was merely that *more* "commonplace" events occurred on one nocturnal program than usual. I didn't resent my duties. But when they stacked up on me, I usually got up in the morning looking and feeling like someone who led a much less circumspect life than my own. All the aftereffects and none of the fun.

One good challenging emergency a night I could take in my stride, but on that occasion everything in the book was thrown at me. The masters were always reminding me of how lucky I was that my children went to bed at eight. Their boys, the upper formers, didn't turn in until nine. My counter-charge was that once a twelve-year-old hit the sack, he was out until someone shook him into sensibility the next morning. The eights and nines, on the other hand, were unpredictable.

I had just got to sleep when a small hand touched my cheek. I flipped on my light. Standing beside my bed was Bobby.

"Oh, gee," he made his empty apologies, "I sure do hope I didn't wake you."

"Oh, my no," I reassured him. "I was still awake."

His hair was tousled and the third button on his wrinkled pajamas was casually latched through the top buttonhole. He was his usual self, except that his face had a pallid, greenish cast. I should have anticipated this particular visit and waited up for it. Bobby always got a stomach-ache after he'd been home for a holiday. He had one—Type II, of course— which took an hour of therapy, plus a change of bed linen, since his attack had "come up" as quickly as it had "come on" him.

I finally flipped off Bobby's light and went back to my bed. I read a few paragraphs of Homer's composition, "The Significance of the Mahabharata in Hindu Literature," in lieu of a sedative. Perhaps Homer's father knew a few interesting facts on this subject, but he obviously hadn't passed on the cream of them to Homer. I dozed off to sleep.

Once more a reluctant small hand tapped me awake. This time it was a disheveled and mournful Winthrop.

"I done it!" he sobbed. "I done it again."

Winthrop always wet his bed after a holiday, but I had got him up and tapped him at ten-thirty and had gone to sleep with a false sense of security. No matter how reassuring I was, he always was traumatized when it happened and in sheer panic that the other boys would discover his weakness. It took fifteen minutes to change his pajamas and his bed— which required turning the mattress—and another half hour of talk to make him comfortable. My technique was so emphatic that night that I suspect Winthrop went off to sleep, smug in the conviction that I also was afflicted with his regressive habit.

I took a second dose of Homer's barbiturate and was just drifting off when loud screams had me out of bed like a bullet and into the corridor—robeless and barefoot. It was amazing how little wear and tear my dressing gown got in my climax-cluttered existence.

Kevin dashed into my arms. "It was just a dream, wasn't it? Just a dream—"

"Of course, it was just a dream," I soothed. I led him into my sitting room and held the shivering child in my arms while his voice shook out the nightmare from his mind. He had dreamed he'd fallen into a dark, deep hole and that his mother looked over the edge and said there was no way of getting him out—so she went away and left him there.

Just telling the nightmare calmed him somewhat—and

fortunately, for I had little time to concentrate on Kevin.

His crying woke up Peter, who decided it was a perfect time to play a trick on the boys and so he ran to his doorway and yelled up and down the corridor, *"Fire! Fire!* Run for your life, men!" Every "man" promptly leaped out of bed to run for his life.

I corralled the stampeding herd in my sitting room. Then every single "man" discovered he was starving to death and wouldn't last the night out. SCIONS OF EIGHT PROMINENT WEST COAST FAMILIES PERISH FROM MALNUTRITION, I visualized the headlines in the Los Angeles *Times.*

"Well—" I tried to keep the tired sigh out of my voice. After all, most children need a snack at an odd hour once in a while. "If you will all be as silent as slinking Indians while I'm gone, I'll hie out into the dark night and seek provisions. You poke up the fire, Larry."

So—I plodded over to the kitchen and lugged back graham crackers and milk. The way they plowed into the food I almost believed that starvation gag.

The show went on its relentless way like a radio serial. Everyone munched his crackers, dropping crumbs all over the floor. Jeffrey and Peter both spilled their milk and promptly, like the thoughtful little helpers they were, mopped it up with their pajama jackets—making it necessary to recostume them for the rest of the act.

Suddenly Jamie looked at the clock and discovered it was three o'clock in the morning. *"Yeeps!"* he cheered. "It's three o'clock in the morning and we're *up!* Isn't that wizard?" One of the Pines had brought back the adjective "wizard" after the holidays and it had already become part of our language.

Peter started *singing,* "It's three o'clock in the morning. We've ate graham crackers the whole night through."

Kevin, completely recovered by this time from his nightmare, said wistfully, "Gee! I always wondered what it was like outside at three o'clock in the morning."

I am a congenital push-over, I suppose. I suddenly remembered that when I was a child I had always wanted to know what the world looked like at three o'clock in the morning, too. I recalled the magical wonder of the time my father whispered me awake one night with the exciting words, "You wanted to see the sky at three o'clock? Well—here we go." He wrapped me in a blanket and carried me out into the crisp, cold early morning. It was high adventure. I was eight years old at the time.

Of course, I couldn't piggyback all the Acorns. Still—they could tiptoe. The night was shot to hell anyway. There was little of it to be salvaged, and tempers were going to be short the next day anyway. "Well, let's see what it looks like," I said.

Everyone put on a robe and slippers and out we crept. It was conspiratorial and fun. They loved it. Of course, nocturnal prowling was not condoned at The Oaks, but I figured that a little rule breaking wasn't excessive indulgence, so long as we were quiet about it and didn't get caught.

The boys were cooperative paragons until Joe's three dogs came bounding across the lawn. I suppose they caught the spirit of the night, too, and said, "Yaps! Three o'clock in the morning and here's a whole bunch of our boys come to play with us." Some fun! They started yipping excitedly and racing around the lawn like a bunch of creatures possessed. Boys and dogs have a strange communicative kinship. Without speech, boys can tell dogs what to do, and similarly dogs can tell boys.

The boys all joined in the moon-mad performance. They leaped and ran for the sheer joy of feeling themselves in motion. Then Peter started barking at the dogs. *"Arf! Arf!"* he

yelped, and before I could muzzle him, all the boys barked.
Then the dogs talked back. Cheerful repartee it was, but
loud.

Suddenly, on flipped Dr. Barrett's light. Before I could
round up and quiet my mavericks, the headmaster was among
us. He looked calm and well groomed, as if he had just show-
ered and slipped into a fresh pair of pajamas and a neatly
pressed robe. In contrast, the ravages of my wild night were
even more blatant. As he stared at me, I felt utterly gauche
and unkempt. Somehow I expected him to shout, in a voice
of doom, "*What* is the meaning of all this?"

Instead, he said to me, "Don't you know that young boys
need their sleep? You should *not* have got them up at this
hour." *Got them up!* I was startled out of my defensiveness.
I brushed at my straggly hair. "Will you please come over to
my study during your free period in the morning? I want to
talk to you." He added a couple of flourishes about the responsibility and dignity of the teaching profession.

"Say, sir, she didn't *get* us up," said Peter. "We got *her* up,
didn't we, guys?"

"Never mind," said Barrett, "this is no time for a tribunal.
All of you, get to bed." He followed them over to the dormitory and gave out a curt "good night" as he witnessed each subdued little renegade crawl into his cot.

As I told Joe that morning, "It's all so awful. These kids
ought to be at home where there aren't so *many* problems,
and where it's legal to give a little leeway to the law. Every
little guy here ought to get the center of the stage once in a
while."

"Well, look, Tootsie, you sure let them all get in the act
last night. Besides, lots of people in the world have eight or
nine children. It's supposed to be dandy."

"Sure, but all eight of them aren't nine years old at the
same time," I reminded him. "After all, there's a special little

spot in the sun for every age and these small ones don't get it."

"I know," Joe agreed. "I'm just trying to whistle our bogey-man away. You're right, everything is either multiplied by eight or divided by eight and never to anyone's advantage. It's the same in my dorm with the twelve-year-olds. School life just *isn't* family life."

It was too true. It worked out that way time and again. Why, in a boarding school a boy doesn't even have a cereal-box top he can call his own so he can send it off to get him-self a Hopalong Cassidy badge.

Take measles—take chicken pox—take dancing school—take baseball—take "awful hard arithmetic problems"—all very important milestones. A conscientious mother and father in the home setting will both give their all to long division right along with Junior when that awesome hurdle appears to test his mental mettle. And, similarly, they'll suffer the social milestones. They will slick down their son's hair, knot his father's best tie around his neck, and fill him to the brim with silken flattery, designed to support his wavering spirits when he strides off to dancing school for the first time.

But in boarding school, I discovered, home-style methods won't work. For instance, though parents can get away with it upon occasion, it is implausible and ineffective for a teacher to tell *each* little boy that he is the most gorgeous male that ever went forth for his first major engagement in the battle of the sexes. Such a sentiment loses its punch after it's repeated eight times. Fancy phrases multiplied by eight become ma-larky. And maternal solicitude divided by eight provides aw-fully short snorts.

I repeat, take measles—take chicken pox—take any com-municable disease. I have heard friends of mine refer to their children's illnesses in a debonair manner. "It's just three-day measles—" or "I put him to bed and treated him like a crown prince for a couple of days and he was okay, but a bit spoiled, of course—" or "You know, chicken pox, it's *nothing.*" Silly women! Nothing contagious is "nothing" in a boarding school. Three-day diseases don't exist. Measles—the so-called three-day variety—turned out to be a forty-day-and-nightmare, by the time everybody who made the catch clocked up his "negligible" allotted three days. Communicable diseases in a boarding school are easier to catch than fish in a barrel.

I suppose Jeffrey Carruthers brought the measles back with him from Palm Springs. That's where he spent his Thanksgiving holidays. He was, I suspect, spotty when his parents deposited him at the school on Saturday night. I remembered afterward that they dropped him like a hot clinker. They didn't even stop the motor or get out of their car. Jeffrey carried his own bags, and his mother called, " 'By, darling," and was off. The Carrutherses were scheduled to leave on a cruise the following Monday, and even a delay for three-day measles would have made them miss their ship. Besides, how can anyone tell from the first eruption whether it's the herald of a three-day or a three-week siege?

The Carrutherses needed their rest. They were *so* tense. They had been packing and unpacking and rushing from Phoenix to Palm Springs and back to Beverly Hills for months. I may be unjust, but I believe that the Carrutherses were knowingly racing their Cadillac that day against the bursting out of the blotches.

When Jeffrey got his full-blown polka dots that night, he mentioned that he had had a few in the morning and his mother had said they were probably from eating too many chocolates. He also conveyed the incriminating information that his parents had planned to drive him over on Sunday but changed their minds when they discovered he'd been over-indulging in sweets. They brought him back a day early to punish him. "Maybe it was measles all along and not candy at all," Jeffrey said. "I guess my mother will be surprised and terribly sorry she didn't keep me home, won't she?"

"Yes, she'll be terribly sorry." Like a hungry boy confronting a banana split, I thought to my cynical self.

Measles can be memorable. It is part and parcel of the proper heritage of childhood that illnesses be taken seriously. I myself remember measles as one of the high points of my ninth year. I ate my favorite foods, my mother introduced me to Mowgli and read to me hour on end, and my father tuned up his old guitar and taught me to sing "You can't get to heaven in a rocking chair." And then, when I went back to school, I bragged about my brush with the Grim Reaper and ornamented myself with a lurid description of my symptoms.

Jeffrey came closest to having measles properly. Being the only sick child in a boarding school is relatively optimum. But the incubation period was fleeting, and all the Acorns got measles. Then every other boy in the school who hadn't had measles took up the fad—one by one. The three-patient infirmary, equipped with all the extra beds it would hold, was reserved for complications such as extremely high temperatures and ear involvements. We got an extra nurse up from Phoenix and I, too, went on full-time duty as a pinch-hitting Flossie Nightingale. We had in the forty days that followed twenty-nine cases of measles.

Homer, with the ingenuity of his kind, figured out statistically how many spots we totaled. His formula, he admitted, was not foolproof, but taking a conservative estimate of five blotches per square inch of body surface, he appraised our total as approximately 352,520 measles. Homer had lots of time on his hands for such fanciful mathematics because his mother generously kept him home during our epidemic. She said to me afterward, "You know, it may sound unfeeling of me, but sometimes I wish Homer were a boarder. I think he regards me as half-witted, and having him around the house all day gives me a terrible inferiority complex." I could sympathize with her. She not only had Homer, she also had Professor Curtis, who was a horse of the same color, only bigger.

I tried to do the right thing by the 352,520 measles. However, the nurse and I found ourselves running from room to room, taking temperatures, pouring orange juice, fluffing pillows, and then dashing on. An eight-year-old with measles, even three-day measles, should be allowed to luxuriate, with the best bedside manners exercised on him, and with good sick-room floor shows presented for his personal pleasure. But there wasn't time.

My conversations, of necessity, were limited pretty much to: "How do you feel, fellow?" "Have you had a bowel movement today?" "Don't scratch, dear." "Now, keep your mouth closed on the thermometer and don't bite it."

During the five minutes of temperature taking, I did tell my patient a funny story which I snatched in passing from a dull-edged collection called *Have You Heard This One?* In every instance, I had, but the boys hadn't. By the time I had traipsed down the corridors, however, and had repeated my witticism twenty times, it palled on me and the true spirit of the storyteller was not in me. I have been somewhat intolerant of pairs of Irishmen and pairs of Scotchmen ever since.

We tried to provide equipment for solitary entertainment. I made the monstrous blunder of buying every boy in my dormitory a kit for building a model airplane. They worked enthusiastically on this constructive play in bed. As a consequence, glue and another high-smelling essential liquid ingredient called "dope" were spilled on clean sheets; measly little aeronautical engineers added to their misery and my nursing duties by cutting their fingers with razor blades; and all beds had to be brushed out twice a day, at least, to clear them of balsa-wood shavings, scraps of tissue paper, thumbtacks, and other odds and ends of industrial refuse.

All my Acorns owned radios, of course, and all favored the same programs. They all tuned their instruments to top volume. If a stranger from Mars had dropped in on our infirmary, he would have assumed that every child at The Oaks had impaired hearing. Even behind a closed door in my own sitting room, I could hear the radios much too clearly for comfort. And as I walked down the hall, "Hi-ho, Silver—" screeched at me from every open doorway. I suggested that perhaps it would be a good idea to have only one radio operating and have it placed halfway down the hall. They all hooted at the proposal as rank heresy.

"We couldn't possibly hear it," Larry protested.

"And what if we got tired and wanted to turn it off?" demanded Bobby. Since I had never known anyone to turn off a radio, Bobby's question struck me as pure filibustering. I shrugged my shoulders and let the radios roar.

Parents were notified promptly when the measles struck their sons. Most of them wrote letters and many of them sent presents. These were usually beautifully wrapped items, selected by professional shoppers in department stores with more eye to profit to their employers than utility to a convalescent. An air rifle arrived for Bobby, and Jeffrey got a fine yew bow, complete with metal-tipped arrows. Both of these lethal instruments *had* to be tested. The life and limb of ambulatory boys were definitely threatened if they got within the range of either Bobby's or Jeffrey's windows from which BB's and arrows catapulted in reckless aimlessness.

Winthrop's mother sent him a beautiful bench-made pair of cowboy boots. Winthrop had been wanting some new boots even before he got measles. He showed little enthusiasm when they finally arrived, however. Instead, he propped them up on his dresser where he gazed at them with baleful resignation. Winthrop, like so many very healthy people, was always unduly concerned when even a minor ailment frustrated his

normal high activity. Just a sniffle or half a degree of temperature convinced him he was not long for this world.

"Lovely boots," I remarked, when I was making my regular
rounds.

"Yeh, they're okay, I guess," said Winthrop wistfully. "I
wrote a poem about them. Afterward, you can send it to my
mother."

"Oh? What is it?"

"Well—this is how it goes." Tragically, he recited:

> All he could do was lie and stare,
> At the cowboy boots he was never to wear.

"You can wear them this afternoon, you know," I said.
"Dr. Grainger told me you are ready to get up."

"I *am?*" demanded Winthrop. "Aw, crap! Say—before I
do it, though, how's about you sending that poem to my
mother and tell her I'm dead? Oh boy, I bet she'd cry!"

I decided I'd better slip this problem to Dr. Grainger. He
was good at treating both the soma and the psyche and Winthrop obviously had a few spots on both at the moment.

No parental present was quite so unique as the one sent
to Jamie. He thought up the idea himself and wrote and
solicited his mother's cooperation. Why she complied I shall
never know. Perhaps she wasn't even at home and the Traverses' housekeeper who, by arrangement, always opened
Jamie's letters when his parents were away, may have followed her mistress's explicit instructions always to send Jamie
anything he said he needed. He didn't *really* need a hypodermic needle, however.

The small air-mailed parcel came in on the afternoon post
and I took it in to Jamie myself.

"Oh, boy!" Jamie said as soon as he saw the package. "I
know what this is, and is it ever *super!*"

"Open it," I suggested. "What is it?"

"I don't know whether I should or not. It's sort of a surprise, kind of, for the boys. Oh, I guess I'll let you in on it," he offered generously. "You'll be *crazy* about it."

He tore off the box's wrappings, and inside, resting on its hygienic cotton, lay a viciously needled hypodermic syringe!

"Why, whatever is it?" I gasped. "It's not a hypodermic needle!"

"Sure is," said Jamie proudly. "See—this is what I'm going to do. I'm going to fill this thing with castor oil and then I'm going to put injections of castor oil in all those oranges I had my mother send." He gestured to a crate of top-grade Sunkists which had been delivered the day before. "Won't that be simply super? It's a perfectly *wizard* idea."

My wayward mind immediately concurred quietly that it was a fairly "wizard" idea, and I gave Jamie a respectful glance, before starting to undermine his diabolical scheme. After all, one can't dose seven small measle victims with castor oil, just for the laughs. Moreover, one can't leave a hypodermic needle in the possession of an imaginative nine-year-old.

"Jamie," I began, "you know what I think would be a better idea. Let's put salt solution in the oranges instead of castor oil. You just want a good joke on the boys—you don't want to make them sick, do you?"

"Don't have to make them sick. They're sick already."

"That's right, they're sick enough, so why don't we get Nurse Johnson to make you up some heavy saline solution and you can jab that into the oranges for the boys?"

"Well—castor oil tastes a lot worse." Jamie was reluctant to forego any of the refinements of his plot. "But I guess salt tastes bad enough." As he talked, he flourished his treasure at me. My already shattered nerves cried their protests.

"Now, Jamie—about this needle," I said tensely, feeling my way carefully into my plotted betrayal. I wanted him to give it to me voluntarily. "You know, you are a very responsible boy and obviously you will take care of that hypodermic needle, but you realize as well as I do that *some* of the Acorns aren't as mature and reliable as you. After all, you are nine now. If you have a hypodermic needle, every boy in this school is going to want a hypodermic needle, and what can I ever do about a thing like that? Imagine Kevin with such a thing!" I had to sell someone down the river for this cause.

"Oh, gosh! Kevin is so clumsy he'd sure hurt himself, wouldn't he? Gee, it's lucky I'm the one that thought this up, isn't it? Me nine now and everything. And I betcha Andy Mansfield—even though he's a great big guy—I betcha he might get mad and just *stick* it in someone!"

"Oh—I never thought of *that!* Oh, you are so wise, Jamie. What do you think should be done with the needle, then? Obviously, lots of boys will want them and some of them might even borrow yours when you're out of your room."

"They *better* not!" said Jamie fiercely, and then wrinkled his brow in a thoughtful frown. "I know what. Why don't you keep it for me in that locked medicine closet of yours? Then no one can get it."

"Why, that's the best idea I ever heard of—it's wizard! I'll do it. You think of *everything*, Jamie."

So Nurse Johnson and I mixed up a heavy dosage of strong salt solution and Miss Johnson filled the syringe and guided Jamie's hand while he injected oranges for all his friends' luncheon trays.

"The queerest goings on I ever saw in my life in this place," Nurse Johnson mumbled under her breath.

The depredation to the oranges didn't show at all. Jamie was right. It was a "wizard" idea—and a little salt never hurt anyone. The plot, as a matter of fact, quite brightened, even for the victims, one of the measle epidemic's duller days. It was diverting for my patients to spend a whole afternoon planning dastardly reprisals.

I don't know when I ever locked up anything as happily as I did that hypodermic needle.

There was only one consolation in our epidemic of measles. "We were lucky, I think," Dr. Grainger said pleasantly, after announcing the victory over our germ warfare.

"Lucky!" I sneered. Doctors are pretty damned cheery about the minor illnesses of the Overprivileged, I decided cynically. They pay off just as well as the major illnesses of the Underprivileged.

"Yes—very lucky. It was just three-day measles, you know," Dr. Grainger explained. "It could have been scarlet fever just as easily." I thought I detected a lustful gleam in his eye. But then I decided that along with the eight pounds and most of my Christian virtues which I had sloughed off during the epidemic, I had also probably tossed off my sense of proportion. For no one was a greater bulwark to me at The Oaks and no one was more understanding and sympathetic to both the physical and emotional needs of the little lonely ones than Dr. Grainger.

After all, it was just three-day measles. Everyone knows that's *"nothing."*

Ten-o'clock Scholar

New boys applying for enrollment after the term's onset were always eyed with a certain amount of suspicious appraisal. Such a ten-o'clock scholar could best justify his irregular status with a few honorable measle scars or a holdover hack from whooping cough.

Otherwise, the ugly question invariably reared its head as to just where the latecomer had been serving his time. It was so very possible that he had already proved himself a thorn in the side of some headmaster and had been bounced from another school. A boy who bounced once was usually like a good India rubber ball—there was a lot of potential bounce left in him. The kiss of death to any reputable boarding school is the rumor of being port of call for incorrigibles. There are some schools, of course, whose business is built on catering to what are politely called "high-spirited lads"—the kind of "boys who will be boys." The Oaks, however, even in the years when tuition was hard come by, made no such dangerous compromises. Once Dr. Barrett was seduced by an impressive Dun and Bradstreet rating and a high I.Q. into accepting, without much sifting of circumstances, a late-October entrant. He turned out to be a typical "boy will be boy" type, a Grade A high-spirited bouncer.

96

His name was Marlin Carrington and he became as legendary as Paul Bunyan. All manner of reckless daring was attributed to him—most of it apocryphal. However, it was substantiated that he set his bed on fire one night from underneath where, uncomfortably cramped, he did his illicit smoking. He also was precocious in other more dangerously pyromaniac ways. He had all the boys afire with interest in some extracurricular anatomy seminars he conducted back of the stables.

Even the favorite, first-born sons of steel tycoons were in the future looked upon with wariness if they applied so much as two weeks late. Proper-minded parents are farsighted in picking boarding schools for proper-minded boys.

However, Mrs. Jackson Cameron's twelve-year-old son, "Jackie Darling," carried no stigmata. He arrived mid-November but with the acceptable purity of motive implicit in snarled marital ties in his family. Jackie Darling seemed a little too sizable for an easy snatch, but Mrs. Cameron was of the opinion that his father might attempt an abduction before Cameron vs. Cameron was heard in court. Understandably, Jackie Darling was a prize piece of community property and, unlike bond and stock certificates, he couldn't be equally divided. Nor could he be liquidated, along with a yacht, a Luscum cabin plane, and some Palomino polo ponies for amenable distribution. Possession being nine points of the law, Mrs. Cameron's object in bringing Jackie to The Oaks was to cache him away. The school's policy under such circumstances was, sensibly enough, to team up with the parent paying the tuition.

Dr. Barrett accepted Jackie, sight unseen. His uncle, Philip Tremont Achison of San Francisco, was a close friend of the Bannisters, who were related to Priscilla Alden, I think, and who had a corner on some excellent radio-hucked commodity, I forget what. Mr. Achison had some ancestors of his own, and an impeccable bank balance besides! He telephoned long distance from San Francisco and Mr. Bannister sent seven genealogical telegrams in which it was clearly pointed out that, although the Achisons weren't able to get passage on the *Mayflower*, they did come over on one of the better boats.

Mr. Achison explained the whole unfortunate situation, mumbling angrily about "that cad—that rotter," invectives that Dr. Barrett with his British orientation understood perfectly. Two days later, Mr. Achison's unhappy, humiliated sister, Mrs. Cameron, and Jackie arrived.

It was not our high rating with the General Education Board that attracted Mrs. Cameron. It was geography. Only a very conscientious and determined kidnaper, she decided, would plot a pilgrimage across a state line and up a mountainside. Mr. Cameron was anything but energetic. Although Mrs. Cameron had driven five hundred miles, preshipped four trunks for Jackie, and had cinched his registration with an advance check for one thousand dollars, she didn't actually surrender him until she went through some properly maternal gestures of concern over the wisdom of her selection. She had a whole battery of pertinent interrogations, and careful instructions for Jackie's care and feeding.

Dr. Barrett had discovered, and admitted, grudgingly, that a woman's word at preliminary conferences with indecisive parents was often persuasive. He frequently invited me into his study to join forces with him in putting the polish on our product. I was supposed to speak, with the authority of my sex, on the superior quality of the school mattresses, how rife with vitamins the diet, the credentials of the dancing-school teacher, what techniques were undertaken to prevent boys with braces from drooling, etc. Upon rare occasion, a "neurotic, anxiety-ridden" parent might even inquire if any attention were given to the love-and-security needs of a small boy.

It was conceded by Dr. Barrett that a woman carried more conviction in such nebulous discussions.

Bobby Lennox was sent to my classroom to summon me to the office the day Jackie Cameron arrived. Bobby was the most satisfying emissary I have ever encountered. He required no prodding cross-examination ever. He always verbalized everything he knew in one prolonged outburst. "Dr. Barrett says for you to have all the second formers go down to study hall. He wants you to come up to his office because there's a new kid here. Yeeps—he's a big guy, too. Betcha he's good at football. Oh boy—they sure got a special-built Cadillac, I'll say! It's neat." Six boys jumped out of their seats and ran to the window. "His name's Jackie and his mother is sure sad about something. She's crying awful. She calls him 'darling' all the time. Betcha it makes him mad. She's sure got red hair, I'll say!"

Bobby was a reliable observer. I entered Dr. Barrett's office fully briefed for what Joe always dubbed "the damp-type character." Mrs. Cameron was a damp type and she "sure had red hair, I'll say!" It hung to her shoulders in a page-boy bob, and its color, though possibly duplicated occasionally by Nature, was in this instance definitely not from the brush of the Old Master Painter. She sat in the large, green leather chair, which was very becoming to her. She wept with a certain quiet charm that was both appealing and adroit. She handled her handkerchief with practiced grace.

"Jackie Darling, stand up, a lady just came in." These were the first words I heard her speak. Her voice was a charming blend—implying Western birth, Eastern finishing school, and an admiration for Katherine Hepburn that got a little out of hand.

Jackie, sitting tensely on the edge of his chair—normal sitting posture for new boys—stood up at her command like a released jack-in-the-box. He was large for twelve, but not

fat—just a big boy who would be bigger one day if the size
of his feet and hands were prophetic of his promise. Topping
his unusual height was a face he must have inherited from
his father. He was blue-eyed and towheaded, in contrast to
his mother, whose red hair might once have been almost anything, and whose eyes were gypsy black. Jackie handled his
recently acquired size with the clumsiness of unfamiliarity.
His face, big-boned like his body, was handsome, but like a
mask with only alert eyes showing through. He was the most
expressionless child I had ever seen—and the sad thing was,
his face was modeled for motility.

"Jackie Darling, shake hands," his mother prompted, following Dr. Barrett's introductions. Jackie thrust forth his dis-
proportionate paw. His mother always cued him before his
line-time had lapsed. She told him when to sit down, and he
did.

"Now—we have something of a problem here," Dr. Barrett
said to me, tapping his pipe against his teeth.

That's no joke, Doc, I thought to myself. Couldn't Jackie
Darling even whip up a nasty sneer for his mother? Ominously Oedipal, I diagnosed.

"Yes, my child and I are in a very grave and threatening
situation," Mrs. Cameron took over.

"This may bore Jack," Dr. Barrett interrupted with no
sublety. "Would you like to go out and have a look at the
gymnasium, Cameron?"

Jack opened his mouth to speak, but the words came out of
his mother. "Oh, it's quite all right to talk frankly in front
of Jackie. He's my big boy now, aren't you, pet?"

"Yeh, I'm pretty big," Jack agreed modestly.

"He's been such a comfort. He's very understanding about
it. Far beyond his years." She paused for a sniffle, nicely muf-
fled by her handkerchief. "Children do grow up overnight
under such circumstances. It's sad but inevitable, I guess.

But better they know the truth than be confused with evasions and half-truths or open lies. Don't you agree, Dr. Barrett? Vishputi thinks so."

"Oh, quite." Dr. Barrett nodded sagely. "Children have much more insight than is usually credited them."

"You're so right," Mrs. Cameron interrupted again. "Now, Jackie knows what I have been through. My dear—you are a woman, you would understand." She turned to me. "It has been quite unspeakable."

"I'm sorry things have been difficult," I sympathized weakly.

" 'Difficult' hardly describes it. And divorces are so degrading—Vishputi feels they are—but what can you do? Vishputi says that, of course, marriage is degrading in the first place—that every man belongs to himself and to himself alone—women, too, he meant."

"Vishputi?" I questioned. Vishputi sounded a bit like a second-string Confucius on a bender.

"Vishputi is a friend and counselor to Mrs. Cameron," Dr. Barrett explained, and put the silencer on me with a frown.

"But even Vishputi agrees with my lawyer that something must be done about the property and everything, you know— and certainly Jackie shouldn't be with anyone except his mother. He belongs to me. That is, I bore him. He belongs to himself, of course, and to himself alone. You can imagine what kind of a woman his father will probably marry if he has his freedom. I couldn't let a woman like that influence Jackie. You see what I mean?"

I didn't have to look far to see what she meant.

"It seems likely that the court will award you the custody," Dr. Barrett reassured her. "It usually works out that way."

"Nothing works out in the usual way where Jackie's father is concerned. He is not beyond kidnaping him and taking him out of the country. Actually, I have brought Jackie here be-

cause I have heard this is a reliable school, and since his father
has no possible way of finding out where he is, I think he
will be safe. Besides, he couldn't possibly land a plane here.
We simply cannot let Jackie be exposed to his father." The
way she put it, Mr. Cameron sounded for all the world like
a communicable disease.

"You can depend upon us to exercise caution, Mrs. Cameron," Dr. Barrett said. "We have on several occasions had
children who were permitted to communicate with only one
parent. We handle it with tact, but firmness. And since Mr.
Cameron doesn't know his own son's whereabouts, I think
there will be no cause for concern."

"Well—we are in a peculiar position. We don't know where
Mr. Cameron is." She gave the room a quick frisk with her
eyes as if she expected him to pop up from behind the sofa.
"He is hiding out apparently until the case comes up—won't
settle outside court, like respectable men do. My lawyer is
outraged—and Vishputi thinks it's crass, too. He'd do anything to get Jackie—just to spite me. He doesn't love him,
not as I do. As Vishputi says, what is there to give beyond
the gifts of a mother—life and love? I've never begrudged
Jackie a thing in my life—have I, pet?"

"Huh-uh," Jackie agreed.

"Jackie Darling, don't say 'huh-uh,' dear—say, 'No,
Mother.'" Jackie repeated it. His face was sober, but
unshadowed with anger. His emotional control was distressing for a twelve-year-old. He revealed no vindictiveness over his father, nor any rebellion over his mother's
verbal sleeve-plucking—a maternal malpractice that is usually protested openly and violently—even by new boys.

Jackie merely sat in polite but stiff attention. A very odd
piece of boy, I decided.

"Jackie is to receive no mail except from me, from his
uncle, from his maternal grandmother, from Vishputi of

course, and from a list of approved friends which I will provide. To safeguard him completely, however, I have hit on an inspirational idea. We will have a password."

"A password?" Dr. Barrett questioned. Oh boy! A password, I thought. Shades of E. Phillips Oppenheim.

"Yes—if anyone with authority to talk to Jackie phones, for instance, he must, even before he identifies himself, whisper the password to you. And only letters bearing the password on the envelope are to be given to Jackie."

"Have you thought up the password?" I asked in breathless fascination.

"Oh yes—'Watson.' Do you get it?"

"Watson? Oh—you mean Sherlock Holmes's friend?"

"Precisely! Vishputi suggested 'Allah,' but my brother is so stolid and unimaginative. He said it was silly and that he refused to write the word or even speak it into a phone. So 'Watson' seemed second best. Not as obvious as Sherlock would be. My brother finally agreed, although he said he didn't understand why he couldn't just say, 'This is Philip Achison!' "

She elaborated her plot by explaining that we, too, must identify ourselves if we phoned her, by whispering 'Watson' before speaking our minds. "That way we have double protection," she explained. "I have a confidential phone number and I'll give it to you." She did, but later on I discovered that she had a distressing habit of demanding a new number from the telephone company each month. She usually forgot to notify us of the change. It would have been difficult to summon her, if Jackie ever *had* been kidnaped.

"Now—that's that. I have a few things I want to ask you, Miss—what is your name? Do the boys eat meat?"

"Eat meat—oh, yes," I said. "At least once a day—usually twice in some form."

"That will have to be changed for Jackie," she announced

firmly. "You do the dietetics and manage the housekeeping, don't you?"

"Not exactly—no—but I do check the menus every Sunday and, being the only woman on the staff, I arbitrate the infrequent differences of opinion among the domestics. I'm pretty good at getting boys' favorite dishes slipped into the menu. Is Jackie supposed to have extra meat?" I could imagine the nutritional demands of that lengthy chassis.

"Oh, no. None! He's on a special diet. You see, this marvelous man we know. He's changed my whole life. He's not Krishna Murti, but he's just as spiritual. We call him 'Vishputi'—not an Indian really, but he lived out there and in Tibet. He embraced yogism. And Jackie Darling and I have taken up the diet, too, and the yogi exercises. They've done wonders—simply wonders. I have the food list here."

She handed it to me. It looked like a reducing diet for a cottontail, plus a few heavy dishes, complete with recipes, such as "Cashew Pistachio Nut Loaf" and "Vito-Veg Ragout."

"Well," I began my protest cautiously. "Some of this may be a bit difficult. The goat's milk—that may be hard to get up here."

"Oh? Well, you can substitute cow's milk, can't you?"

"Why, yes—I could do that." Imagine such radicalism.

"Jackie Darling's awfully adaptable. He'll drink cow's milk."

"Are you willing to drink cow's milk?" I asked Jackie. I wanted to squeeze a few words out of him, if there were any there.

"I think I can stand it," he said, "if it isn't cold and doesn't taste too good." If I had thought up those lines myself, I would have lifted a brow when I said them, but not Jackie. He was as deadpan as a clean skillet. Still, even though he apparently had no sense of humor, it was comforting that he could compose a whole sentence on his own.

"Now," Mrs. Cameron said, "I want to tell Dr. Barrett a few things about Jackie's personal problems. How about you going out to look at the gymnasium now, darling?"

Any right-minded child would have balked. Most boys don't want their "personal problems" discussed at all, but if it is inevitable, they will stay in the arena until they are dragged out.

Jackie arose immediately and his expression still didn't change. I felt like poking him—or her. "Maybe I ought to call Gram," he said. "I told her I'd phone, you know, and tell her how I liked the place."

"Oh, do call Gram, darling," Mrs. Cameron urged. "You're so thoughtful, angel."

I walked out with Jackie. Thoughtful boys usually bore me—but Jackie was a new item on my roster. He didn't bore me but he certainly baffled me. He was a challenge to my insatiable curiosity.

"Where is there a phone?" he demanded as soon as we left the office.

"You can phone from my room if you want to," I offered. "Or do you want to see the school first?"

"I think I'd better phone first." He suddenly seemed alive. There was color in his cheeks.

I led him to my apartment and showed him the telephone. "Can I help you get the connection?" I offered. After all, with an incompetent like Jackie Darling, it seemed likely that telephoning would be a major undertaking.

"Oh, no, thanks," he said. He frowned slightly. "I can do it all alone—and you don't even have to stay here. You probably have lots of things you want to do." He said it pleasantly enough, but I know the brush-off when I get it.

"I'll go in and tidy up." I accepted my dismissal and went into my bedroom and brushed my hair—a luxury I rarely had time for. It wasn't really eavesdropping, because certainly I've never encountered a code of ethics anywhere that disapproved listening to a young boy talking to his grandmother. Actually, I didn't listen. It was just that my walls were thin, and I heard.

"Get me San Francisco Regent 5-011, and reverse the charges, please. I'll hold on." Well—efficient! Who would have suspected it? The connection came through fairly fast.

"Hi," he said, and the animation that was so devastatingly and tragically missing from his face a few minutes before was concentrated in his eager voice. "Yep," he said, "it's me. It's Jackie *Darling.*" There was no longer any doubt in my mind as to how he regarded his impossible title. With mature and tolerant amusement, he flipped the phrase to limbo. "I'm okay. The school is okay. Gee—don't worry about me. Yeh— I miss you, too. I can hardly wait until I see you again—we'll fish the Rogue, huh?"

Well! Good for Grandma, I thought! Then my hand holding my hairbrush froze in mid-air. I stepped closer to the wall.

"And you can write me—it's perfect! All you have to do is put 'Watson' on the letters. It's a password. Anything with 'Watson' on it is okay, get it? And send me some chow— *salame* and pickled herring and stuff that won't spoil. Put 'Watson' on the box. I'm still eating hay, but the dame that fixes the feed bag here looks like an easy mark."

So! The dame that fixes the feed bag is an easy mark! You'll eat those words, Chum, right out of the feed bag!

". . . Oh gee, yeh, I'll write and don't worry. I been nice to her and did just what you told me. Yep, I'll do good work. . . . Yeh, I'll be happy. . . . Sure . . . I can still laugh—" With that he burst into tears.

By this time I had my ear right up against the wall. Ethics be damned! But shortly afterward, he *did* laugh.

"It's red now—Vishputi says she *vibrates* to red. Sure, she'll get over it like the other time. . . . You're right, she is kinda cute and us guys, we do have to take care of her."

I waited quite a while after the receiver clicked before coming out. Did I or didn't I hear this conversation? With an agreeable conscience like mine, it's easy to let it do the guiding.

"I hope I didn't keep you waiting," I said. "Did you get your grandmother?"

"No," he said, and I noted that as he spoke he quickly hooked his middle finger over his first finger—a boy of honor. "I guess she wasn't home." And he looked so pleased about it, I decided he probably didn't really want to talk to his grandmother anyway.

Jackie Darling had insight. The "dame that fixes the feed bag" was a very easy mark indeed.

CHAPTER ELEVEN

Beau Gestures

Directly across the small, stone-paved patio in the same building which housed the Acorns were the school classrooms and administrative offices. It was very convenient getting to class and back to our quarters. However, my little boys always complained of our proximity to the headmaster's study. They felt that this unfortunate geography was all that constrained them from leading recklessly lawless lives. Danger is man's element, so they say, and I discovered that man begins to seek, or invent, his element at a very tender age.

I don't endorse Sin, of course—not a blanket endorsement anyway—but for me to accept with awed admiration my flock's lurid evaluation of themselves made for a certain amount of rapport between us. It proved very useful in guiding them subtly into approved behavior. Since I supposedly acknowledged the fact that they were a bunch of restrained rakes, they usually confided in me the wicked things they'd decided *not* to do.

Corollary with this, and much more useful to me in channeling major traffic into the straight-and-narrow path, they also usually confided the things they *intended* to do. Some of their projected mischief was fascinating and, frankly, quite appealed to my worse nature. It was, alas, my responsibility to restrain
108

them occasionally. I think they sensed my reluctance. To console me for my unfortunate role in life and to assure me they knew what I suffered from my occupational disease, they usually gave up their reign-of-terror plans cheerfully enough. They felt, I am sure, that if I hadn't been on the payroll I'd have been right in there ringleading castor oil into the salad dressing and garter snakes into everyone's bureau drawers. It may not have been a dignified reputation, but it was a mighty handy one, diplomatically speaking. Usually a lurid description of projected depredation gave them all the release they needed anyway. They were often, I think, relieved that I saved them the necessity of execution and still maintained the distinction of their self-appraisal as recruits of Satan.

It gave them some pleasure, too, to oblige me. I remember Jeffrey Carruthers put their whole philosophy in an acorn shell. "It's sure good of us kids to be good, isn't it?" he said. Of course, goodness is relative and, in the case of little boys, a quite distant relative.

I tried to be fair-minded, of course, and the Acorns appreciated this fact. We often contrived a workable compromise between sheer destruction and dull conformity. So—because I cooperated with the boys when I honorably could, they returned the favor and cooperated with me—when they honorably could. This left them quite some leeway. However, I must say in justice to them, they were as good as little boys need to be, to be good little boys.

The Acorns' favorite deviltry, of course, was pretty innocuous, although it was politic not to emphasize its harmlessness, lest they feel challenged to devise something more hazardous. They simply doted on equipment designed to shoot water on people or scare them with sudden noises. They weren't far removed chronologically, you see, from the thrill of leaping out from behind a door and yelling "Boo!"

I had gradations of permissiveness about these things. I

exercised my veto on turning on the sprinkler system when there were forty boys in their best clothes, plus twice as many parents, sitting on the lawn watching Commencement exercises. However, I did permit the use of those irresistible trick devices for shooting thin sprays of water on people. Water pistols, of course, did not fall into this category, being orthodox artillery used in straightforward man-to-man warfare against adversaries similarly armed. The drench dealers of practical jokery were much more subtle devices—rubber boutonnieres, equipped with concealed waterworks, and rings, backed up with water-filled rubber balls, held ready in the hand to squirt any mental incompetent who was balmy-brained enough to smell an Acorn's "pretty flower" or look at his "new ring."

The boys loved this sort of thing. It rolled them in the aisles. But equally they were entertained by inflicting sudden loud noises on unprepared ears. I put few restrictions on noises. It took great ingenuity to create a sound that was sudden enough and loud enough to make any impression whatsoever on the normal environmental uproar of the place. Still, they were resourceful, and when they all got together on the problem, even yelling "Bang!" in chorus was fairly effective.

I felt it wasn't cricket to saw one leg off of each of the dining-room chairs, and without much personal regret I convinced them that pasting all the pages of chapel hymnals together wasn't so sharp. I also, unrued, dissuaded them from substituting salt in all the sugar bowls to "surprise the boys" when they plowed into their breakfast porridge. Occasionally, however, I had to beat myself into marshaling the moral stamina essential to my position as referee. Downcast, with my own disappointment, I discouraged what was probably the most magnificent piece of diabolical ingenuity they ever concocted. By dint of much patient effort over a lengthy period of time, they managed to bring back alive about two hundred assorted moths. They incarcerated their game in ventilated quart Mason jars. They stored these "canned" moths on their closet shelves and, according to Bobby Lennox, fed them every day on ravelings from old worn-out wool socks. Some of them died, of course, from malnutrition, I suppose, or cramped housing, but a vast swarm survived.

This was one instance in which I regretted the rapport I had achieved with the Acorns. It would have been so much more interesting had they executed their insect warfare first and confided in me later. They planned to let loose in Dr. Barrett's tidy closet—for a free-for-all picnic on his well-tailored English tweeds and flannels—this wool-gathering battalion. Dr. Barrett was to be away three days on business in Los Angeles and the attack was scheduled for this brief span when his ramparts were unwatched.

Anyway, and alas!—they told me. My virtue, of course, went unrewarded. Ignorant, completely, of my great spiritual struggle, eight little boys unknowingly witnessed me at my highest pitch of nobility. I explained to them soberly that a joke was a joke only when it did not involve destruction of property. I backed up my middle-class morality with a sound economic argument. I added the practical flourish that, discovered, the Acorns would probably have their allowances garnished for countless years while they financed Barrett's accumulation of a new wardrobe. Such dire possibility of insolvency gave them pause.

Homer, in fact, figured out exactly how many candy bars and ice-cream cones one tweed jacket represented. "Say it cost sixty dollars," said Homer. "That's twelve hundred candy bars. Divide that by eight. That's one hundred and fifty candy bars apiece and, mind you, just for one coat."

"Oh, jeepers!" gasped Bobby. "By the time we bought Dr. Barrett new suits and everything, I guess we couldn't have any candy until we were old men."

"Oh, gosh!" Jeffrey sighed. "Probably we'd have no teeth or anything by that time either."

"I won't bother to go into the lack of logic in that," said Homer with scorn.

"No," I said gratefully, "there's no point in going into it, Homer."

"But what will we ever do with all these moths?" Peter wanted to know. "We got them. Now we ought to use them."

"Couldn't we maybe just put one of them every day in Barrett's closet?" Bobby suggested a compromise. He felt, I am sure, that the moths, too, were going to be disappointed and deserved a few consolation nibbles of the promised imported cheviot.

"Or we could let them all out in chapel on Sunday, maybe, huh?" proposed Jamie.

"Huh-uh, that's not such a good idea," Peter scoffed. "It would make Jesus mad, and, besides, even though the moths know us, they might eat our suits by mistake instead of the other kids' suits." Little boys are amazingly practical in their ethical principles.

"Well, I betcha Jesus would have thought it was funny, too, when he was a boy to have all those moths in Dr. Barrett's closet," Jamie argued in his reluctance to abandon the projected picnic.

"That's blasphemy," announced Homer piously. Trust Homer to have a three-syllable word on tap. "Besides, the people in Jesus' environment wore only linen. It was hot in the Holy Land. It wouldn't have occurred to Jesus to put moths in anyone's closet under the circumstances."

"Heck—what's Jesus got to do with all this?" demanded Jeffrey, sensibly enough. "What are we going to do with the moths?"

The ecclesiastical digression gave me a chance to organize

my thinking. "Let's make moth collections," I suggested. This appealed.

Since it would have been unthinkable for the boys to undertake the mass euthanasia essential to our project, I got Joe to administer the lethal anesthesia. A few of the more spectacular moths had already been given names. A little boy can swat an anonymous insect with savage delight. Cold-bloodedly, however, to obliterate a speckled beauty named (for what reason I can't imagine) "Mr. Beezlebottom" was something else again. To do in Mr. Beezlebottom, who had lived on one's closet shelf and been nourished on one's own personal socks would have put such death dealing on the level of fratricide. It was untenable.

During Dr. Barrett's absence from the school, every first and second former mounted a collection of moths on cork sheets. Homer already knew the genetic names of some of the moths and he quite willingly filled in the blank spots in his knowledge by scholarly research. Homer wanted no blank spots.

Most of the boys laboriously printed below each specimen, "*Tinea pellionella*," etc.

Peter, with a casual disregard of bloodlines, however, settled for "Mr. Beezlebottom, Mrs. Beezlebottom, Bobby Beezlebottom, Betsy Beezlebottom, Business Partner of Mr. Beezlebottom, Bobby Beezlebottom's Flying Teacher," etc.

Dr. Barrett noticed the moth collections on his first day back at The Oaks. He was impressed. He requested that they all be brought to study hall and put on display. During assembly, the next morning, he devoted half an hour to a constructive lecture, lauding the ingenuity, energy, and intellectual curiosity which had motivated the first and second formers in their accomplishment.

"Some of you older boys can profitably pattern your independent activities by the example set by our first formers."

He turned to Peter, who was the elected leader of the Acorns and thereby their official spokesman. "Who thought up this splendid project?" he asked. "What prompted you to start collecting moths?"

"Well—you see—" Peter hesitated and looked very embarrassed and uneasy.

"Don't be modest," Dr. Barrett prodded. "Perhaps you thought up the idea yourself, Peter?"

"Well—not exactly—no, it was like this, see. I guess everyone just decided all at once, sort of, that catching some moths was a good idea."

A mere breath of a chorused sigh of relief came from the Acorns. Even I clocked up our Peter as the diplomat par excellence.

"Splendid!" Dr. Barrett praised. "A thoroughly cooperative venture. And did you all have a good time making these collections, boys?"

"Yes, we sure did, sir," piped all the little paragons. This was no lie. The anticipated diabolical purpose back of the moth collecting had transformed the drudgery into zestful carnival.

"This is an apt example of the fact that teamwork is as much fun and just as effective in intellectual pursuit as it is in sports. How would you all like to go into Flagstaff on Saturday for lunch and a movie?"

The structure of boyhood's code still remains an enigma to me. The unorthodox silence from his cohorts reinforced Peter's own sentiments, I suppose. He spoke up, "I don't think so, sir. I guess us kids better not go. We're planning on catching a few more moths on Saturday. We want to find a—a what you call it, Homer? You know, Mrs. Beezlebottom's brother-in-law."

"None of those Beezlebottoms are even related," Homer answered with scorn. "*Lepidoptera,* you mean."

"Yep, one of them. That's what I mean," Peter said.

"What's the matter—you little twirps all got holes in your heads?" whispered Andy Mansfield.

No Acorn raised voice in protest. How angelic can angels get? How heroic can heroes be? Perhaps they hadn't paid the Piper his full fee, but they were certainly making a saint-worthy gesture.

When we walked out of Assembly, the Acorns all gravitated in my direction. They were all very sober.

"Say, sir," Peter finally spoke with some puzzlement. "That turned out sort of funny after all, didn't it?"

"Very *very* funny," I agreed, and all my suppressed laughter burst forth. Suddenly everyone started laughing. They were hysterical. They screamed and hit each other, until finally Peter gasped, "I'm laughing so hard I'm going to wet my pants."

"Me, too!" said Kevin.

They broke up the huddle to race to the bathroom.

A sudden mist of worry fogged my cheer. Was it normal for little boys to sacrifice a Saturday movie to inflict self-punishment for intentions they had never carried out? For honor and praise they hadn't actually earned? Why, they were being downright—what was it psychologists called it?—masochistic, that's what! Goodness, they'd probably all be compulsively virtuous from now on. I sat at my desk in the English classroom worrying, but enjoying the momentary respite, while I waited for them.

All was quiet. They were a minute late. Suddenly the two doors of the room burst open. Four little boys leaped in one doorway and four in the other. Perfectly synchronized they all yelled, "Bang! Bang!" They looked like a covey of cherubim, but I knew better. They were a band of blackhearted bandits. I was, of course, *simply* terrified!

They walked to their desks and sat down.

"Say, sir, I know an awfully funny new joke. Can I tell it before we start class?" demanded Jeffrey.

"Yes, let's hear it," I said. I felt benign toward all of them.

"Well, see," Jeffrey began. "See—I say, 'I'm a gold lock,' and then you say, 'I'm a gold key'—and like that. Get it? Everything I say, you say the part about the key. Okay?—I'm a gold lock."

"I'm a gold key," I responded obediently, even though I'd been fall guy for this "new" joke about twenty-odd years before.

"I'm a silver lock," said Jeffrey.

"I'm a silver key," I said.

"I'm a monk lock," said Jeffrey.

"I'm a monk key," I obliged. "Oh *my!*"

"She's a *monkey!* . . . Are you a monkey, sir? . . . Oh, what you said!" The boys screamed with delight.

"You aren't really a monkey," Kevin put in gently. "That's just a joke." Kevin always felt the necessity to soothe people's possible wounds.

"Oh, you mushmouth, Kevin. Dry up. She *knows* it's a joke," said Peter. "Now, listen—can I tell a swell riddle before we begin?"

"All right," I agreed, "since I am just a monkey, what would my opinion be worth anyway?"

"Well—this is really a wonderful riddle. There were these three boys, see, named Hit-me, Slap-me, and Sock-me. They were all riding a horse and Hit-me and Slap-me fell off. Who was left?"

"Sock-me," Jeffrey answered brightly.

"Okay," said Peter. He leaped out of his seat, folded his fist, and socked Jeffrey. Everyone thought this was so monstrously clever they decided to write a letter to the Marx Brothers and let them in on it.

Even Jeffrey was a good sport, and laughed. However, for the sake of his honor, he got up and hit Peter back.

"Hit-me, Slap-me, and Sock-me." Bobby savored the delightful words, rehearsing them under his breath for future use. Jamie caught the cue, however. So Jamie hit, slapped, and socked Bobby. The gauntlet was down. Bobby pitched into his aggressor. The smell of a free-for-all was in the air. In two minutes I'd have a riot on my hands.

I raised my voice to the level of authority. "Call out the Marines!" I shouted.

This was an established phrase and meant I'd had enough and back-to-business was the order of the day.

The terrorists relaxed.

"Open your books," I said, "to page seventy."

Obediently, they thumbed the pages.

"Yah—I hate punctuation," announced Peter belligerently.

"Me, too, I hate commas and periods and colons, and semicolons and quotation marks and all that slop," agreed Jamie.

"Punctuation is essential to clarification of meaning," announced Homer.

"Phooie!" Jamie countered automatically.

"It sure would be awful funny if some night a robber got in this school and just simply robbed the place of every single solitary English book there ever was," said Bobby dreamily.

"Say—you know, that *would* be funny," said Peter, and reached over and nudged Jamie and gave him a wink as broad as a bad intention about to burst to full flower.

The mist of worry lifted. I wasn't going to need wing clippers, after all. Normalcy seemed to have a firm seat on the situation.

CHAPTER TWELVE

Music Hath Power

I suppose as a toddler even Jascha Heifetz learning to bow was something of a bore. Still, I imagine that little Jasch showed some tiny spark that consoled his parents during that period of great travail when he was getting the hang of the violin. I hand it to the Heifetzes for holding on. Still, I wager they didn't have their perseverance tested with twenty assorted offspring all doing scales on twenty assorted instruments very badly, and simultaneously. Only on teachers is that particularly excruciating torture inflicted. And believe me, it's rare to the vanishing point for even an approximation of a young Heifetz to show up among the musical tyros in a boarding school. Maybe it's a matter of cause and effect— probably parents don't mind hearing talented tykes practice, and keep them at home. Sandy Spencer was a truly gifted boy but he was a day student and didn't routinely contribute the enjoyment of his accomplishment to our meager fare. His mother was no fool. She had him practice before school every morning to keep him as uncontaminated as possible by his enforced exposure to *our* musicians.

Most boarding schools require that children bring with them twelve cotton underdrawers, clearly marked with Cash's woven name tapes, and vast quantities of other clearly marked assorted necessities. They also recklessly label "Desirable but not Essential": saddles, bridles, sports equipment, cameras, hobby materials, musical instruments, etc. It is a sad commentary on the boarding-school set that nearly all of them have the nonessential desirables, including silver-mounted saddles, and the very noisiest musical instruments money can buy.

No apparent purpose activates selection of instruments unless it's long-plan persecution. The families toward whom I directed the bulk of my ire were those who believed in freedom of choice. Give a nine-year-old boy his head and he can, without a moment's hesitation, pick a weapon twice as lethal as one carefully pondered for months by a parent. Parents will usually settle for piano, but boys always reckon on refinements of torture. Their natural choices in musical armament run to cornets, slide trombones, saxophones, and even violins. For true delicacy in crucifixion, the violin, small size, in the hands of a boy, small size, has no rival. I'll even take percussion to strings any day. A kettle drum is a barbiturate compared to a fiddle.

Little boys always want to take music lessons until they start taking music lessons. If a boy were at home when the urge to shift arts hit him, he could probably get quick permission from his parents to burn up his violin. In fact, the parents might very well beat Junior to the punch and tactfully distract him from Music or, less tactfully, bash the infernal instrument over his head and traumatically shock him into substituting some more constructive "busy hands" work, like basket weaving.

But when a boy goes to boarding school, he is deposited with a lot of equipment and a set of instructions from parents —and alas, the school is pledged to carry out the instructions.

"Here is Christopher." I remember shivering as I heard one departing Mother make her pronouncement. "He has his violin and he is to practice an hour every day and have two lessons a week."

Christopher was really a pleasant little Puck, but at that point one of Charles Addams's diabolical little rogues, arriving with a pet Gila monster, would have been preferable. And there was no percentage in writing a formal protest to parents, pointing out that perhaps money was wasted in giving Christopher a musical education. It's categorical that at a distance *all* children are remembered tenderly by their parents as highly talented. Mary and Warren James were our faculty musicians and they made a pretty penny every month out of this parental aberration. Mary taught piano and Warren band instruments. Once a week, Rodney Romans, a violin teacher from Phoenix, visited the school to promote the torture techniques of strings.

After about three days—possibly a week for a naïve lad—the discovery was always made that boys who did *not* take music lessons had "free time" during the practice hour. Free time was as highly coveted at The Oaks by boys as it was by teachers. There were very few minutes in the day that managed to slip through the rigid iron grillwork of the inviolable schedule. This put an extra touch of unpleasantness in the whole practicing procedure. It was done from then on with resentment. A resentful boy violinist, I might say, is even worse than a happy boy violinist trying his noble best.

I soon discovered just how crafty Joe Hargrave had been in palming off the piano on me. I never touched it—except to dust the top occasionally. Diego, the Mexican houseboy responsible for cleaning our dormitory, apparently had blurred vision or got dizzy spells when dusting furniture higher than a table. Joe was right—our schedule was such that I had to choose between piano playing and bathing. I felt obliged to choose the latter.

One hour a day was set aside for practicing. However, this arrangement accommodated only the portable instruments.

If your ears could stand that one hour a day, it was over and done with, as far as violins, saxophones, slide trombones, French and other un-American horns, kettle drums, etc., were concerned. But the pianos, alas, were something else again. There were only two of them. One was in the main lounge, and one was in *my* sitting room. These pianos had to be shared, of course. So—individuals' schedules were shifted around so that every boy with that sort of evil intent in him could express it on one or the other instrument every day. From eight to five my piano was bangingly busy. Fortunately, I was out of my quarters a good share of the time teaching classes, but I was there enough to have the works of John Williams, and others of his diabolical ilk, forever burned into my memory. I can talk music intelligently with anyone— anyone under ten.

Kevin Clark was in *Book Two—Simplified Classics for the Beginner*. It was he who had finally reached and mired himself in the "Minuet in G." He could be more downright irritating with a piano than anyone I have ever known. Every time he made a mistake, he started again at the beginning. Tra la— *la* la *la* la *la* la—tra la *la*—I hate minuets to this day. I hate white wigs. I hate crinoline. I hate historical novels of the period of the minuet. I even hate the letter *G*.

But here is the paradox. I loved Kevin Clark. I still do, wherever he may be—and how I wonder! There was no lethal purpose back of *his* playing. Kevin's motivations were always of the best.

I remember the time I first saw him. He was presented to me, along with his mother, Mrs. Byrne-Masterson, on opening day. He looked like a starving Greek child that someone with Mephistophelian humor had dressed up in a spectacularly perfect English flannel suit.

He had a look of undernourishment of the body and of the heart. He was a dispossessed waif. He was mute evidence of

Mrs. Byrne-Masterson's youthful matrimonial recklessness. She had been married three times since her first husband, the inconsiderate Mr. Clark, had implanted the frail seed of Kevin. Kevin's hair stood up in a peak over his left eye. That first day his mother pointed it out. "Curious," she said, reaching out to push it flat, "his father had a cowlick in exactly that place." It sounded like an affront, and Kevin held his hand over his hair. Even in class, he had a nervous mannerism of smoothing back his cowlick.

Kevin always tried desperately and defeatingly to adhere to the pattern of grace and accomplishment expected of him. His manners were impeccable. He rose when ladies came into the room, he removed his little Eton cap in elevators, he seated ladies at table, and he said the right things when introduced. But his voice always trembled with apologetic nervousness. He knew subconsciously that he was no adornment to his beautiful mother and that he was, metaphorically, stowed into an old box, like the costume jewelry she had packed away at the time she married Roderick Masterson, who could afford the real pearls her neck deserved. On a whim, she occasionally wore a piece of costume jewelry, if it were amusing enough, and on a similar whim she occasionally wore her maternalism, which was as synthetic as the junk jewelry.

Holidays, Kevin was collected by a chauffeur, an Irishman, named James Patrick Edward Terrance O'Mallory, but called "Mac." "Because I drove a cab for so many years," he explained. Mac was the most stable element in Kevin's life, and even *he* was saving up to go back to Ireland to visit his "old mither in County Cork." Kevin always greeted Mac, upon his arrival at the school, with the frightened question, "How much you got saved now, Mac?"

Kevin wanted terribly to please his mother because he was fairly young to face the world alone. He wanted someone to help him out a little until he got to be—oh say, ten, at least.

So he flung himself into everything with the wild hope of gaining her admiration and love. He plunged into games with a violence that was invariably rewarded with scarred knees and no prestige. He was ill coordinated to start with, and his tense overeagerness tightened his muscles into perverse unresponsiveness to the frenzied dictates of his brain. In the classroom, although he was bright, his efforts were often similarly frustrated. He always broke his pencil in the middle of a spelling test because he clutched and pressed it so hard. Socially, too, he was a dud. He gave boys presents all the time—bought them candy with his allowance. But here, too, his tense, unrelaxed eagerness netted him little return.

Music was no more rewarding to his frantic hopefulness.

It was at the time that Mrs. Byrne-Masterson took her fifth flyer to become Mrs. Phillip Standish and was on her honeymoon that Kevin got into serious trouble.

Kevin came in to practice one Thursday. It so happened that Kevin's practice hour fell during my "free period," so I always got the full bombastic brunt of it. I usually lured the child away from his dedicated duty for part of the hour. I had two reasons for this irregular behavior. One was that even Griselda couldn't have taken the first three bars of the "Minuet" day after day without blowing her patient top. My other reason for enticing Kevin away from the piano was that I always devoted part of the hour attempting to infuse a little light into the cold, dark corridors of loneliness that he inhabited.

Any boy but Kevin would have cooperated with me in my distraction techniques and then would have whooped off to brag to his pals. "Yeeps!" he'd say. "Did I ever work her? She got to talking about when she was a kid and I just kept her going and I didn't have to practice more than fifteen minutes. She never even knew the difference."

But Kevin always got anxious. He actually *wanted* to learn the "Minuet in G."

On that fatal Thursday, he was making more mistakes than ordinarily and the intent expression on his face was more deeply creased into his forehead.

Finally I interrupted and called him over to sit beside me on the sofa. "Will you hold this book while I paste the cover?" I contrived all manner of jobs to get him close to me. Repairing books was as good as any.

"I'll help you, but I better hurry," he said. "I want to learn my piece exactly right before next Monday."

"Oh?" I questioned. "What's happening Monday?"

"My mother is coming here, and she got married and he's coming, too, to see me. I got the letter here." He pulled it out of his pocket and handed it to me. It was creased and re-creased into a little hard wad. I unfolded it.

. . . . So—for goodness' sake, Kevin, be clean on Monday, wear your navy-blue suit, and be a little gentleman because Phillip is so eager to meet you. He wants to be a real father to you, and we don't want him to be disappointed, do we, darling? You be ready to play your piece for him, and I told him you were taking boxing lessons. You and one of your little friends can show him how you can box. . . . I hope you are not as thin as you were. You make Mummy proud of you, and maybe we'll let you go to Canada with us this summer instead of sending you to Camp Alamoso. Phillip said he'd like to take you fishing with him. . . .

"See—I got to learn the piece better." He sounded desperate. "I'm not very good at it. See—it says that he might take me fishing. Do you think he would? I've got a spot on my navy-blue suit—it's catsup, I think, and the coat's wrinkled." He caged up his sobs by setting his lips firmly.

"Oh, Kevin," I said, "you are such a nice boy." I put my arms around him. Barrett and Bad Form be damned!

"Kevin," I said, "this Phillip person will love you, and he won't care a snap whether you can play the piano or not."

"But the boxing—that's no good either. I really want to play the piece."

"Look, Kevin," I said, "I'll spot and press your suit; and as for this piano business, we'll fix that. I'll show you how to lick the 'Minuet.' You simply *mustn't* stop when you make a mistake. Go right on—now listen—"

I sat down at the piano and I played the simple version of the "Minuet in G" and included every error I'd ever heard Kevin make, but I played right through to the end, ignoring them. "How did that sound?" I asked him.

"Oh, that sounded wonderful!" said Kevin. "But you can play better than I can."

"Maybe I *can* play better than you, Kevin, but I wasn't playing better then. I might even have been playing a little *worse* than you do. It was *full* of mistakes." This was no way to train a child—but who cared? "Sit down, Kevin. Play it through and don't stop for *anything*."

He began: Tra la—*la* la *la* la *la* la *la*. Then he paused as usual.

"Go on, Kevin, go on—don't stop!" Prodded by me, he played it through from start to finish.

"That's all right, Kevin. You'll have to go a bit faster, that's all, but pay no attention to mistakes. Just play fast, and keep on. Try it again." He did it.

He looked hopeful. When the bell rang, he ran over and threw his arms around me. "Oh, gee, thanks," he said. It was the first time he had ever been brave enough to show his feelings spontaneously.

I had no notion just how deeply this temporary spirit of freedom had dug into him, however. He went out. Apparently feeling a new sense of strength and hope, endowed by the facility of his pseudo accomplishment, he walked right up to Bob Munsey when he met him in the hall.

"Say, sir, could you help me get my boxing good by Monday? My mother and my new father are coming and she wants me to box someone so he can watch me do it. Could you, sir?"

Munsey was surrounded at the time by six or seven of his followers, older boys at the age when athletic prowess was the epitome of accomplishment. Teddy Lane was also a bystander and it was from him that I later got a full account of what happened.

. Munsey stood for a minute and stared at Kevin silently. Then turning to go, he shrugged his shoulders and said, "Listen, Clark, between now and Monday I couldn't teach you to knock down a canary. Buddy Boy, you'll never box, if you try a million years."

Kevin, according to Teddy, doubled up his fingers, brushed back his cowlick with a fist, and then plowed into Munsey. He rammed his head into Munsey's stomach and at the same time pummeled him with his fists. The incident would probably have been considerably less significant except for one unfortunate circumstance. Munsey had just turned to walk away. He was not only slightly unbalanced in posture but he was completely unprepared for the sudden onslaught. He sat down.

The indignity of his position apparently enraged him. He leaped to his feet and grabbed Kevin. "Why *you*—you—little brat!" he snarled. "You know what you've done? You struck a master!" Munsey, holding Kevin with one strong hand, used the other to slap the boy across the face.

Six hero-worshipers witnessed this gesture. None of them said anything but a chorused sigh came from them—a blend of fright, awe, identification, cruelty perhaps—and certainly disillusionment, in the case of Tim McNeill, anyway. Tim doubled his fists into hard hunks and took two steps toward Munsey. Then he released his fingers. "That little kid was just mad, sir—I'd like—I'd like to hit you, too." Tears came to his eyes and he turned on his heels and hurried away—a former hero-worshiper.

Munsey watched Tim walk away. Tim was The Oaks' Top Boy. His grip on Kevin loosened. Then the anger, heightened by Tim's rejection, returned to his voice. "Clark, come with me," he commanded. He led him toward Barrett's office. Kevin, by this time, realized the monstrousness of what he had done. Between gasped sobs he reiterated his regrets. "I didn't mean to—I didn't mean to—I'm sorry—don't tell my mother —I didn't mean to—I'm sorry."

They brushed by Joe on their way.

"What's up?" Joe asked.

"This boy struck me," said Munsey, and kept on moving.

"Hurt you bad?" Joe said. Munsey didn't bother to answer. He and Kevin disappeared into the study.

Even if Teddy hadn't told me what happened, I'd have caught the overtones. The grapevine in a school operates with flashing speed. Words were whispered behind books in every classroom the next hour—and the emotional context of the words was obvious. Kevin Clark had finally made a dramatic impression on his peers.

"You know what—that little old kid, Kevin Clark—he knocked Mr. Munsey down. . . ." "Yep, just hit him one— and *down* he went!" . . . "That little guy—not nine yet— he just hit him. One pookey-boo and boy! he fell right over. . . ." "Gee—imagine it! What'll they do to Kevin?" . . . "Tim McNeill, he's on the kid's side—he saw it all. . . ." "So's Teddy Lane."

Kevin had English with me that hour. He came into class late, looking like a sad little mole hunting for a hole into which to scamper. All his brave momentary vindictiveness was gone. He handed me a note. It was from Barrett.

Kevin Clark is on probation. He is to follow his regular schedule except for playtime, which he will spend in his room. His case will be reviewed in Faculty Meeting Friday night.

The next morning, Kevin came to breakfast, ate everything on his plate like a good boy, and then threw it all up.
He apparently showed up for Leonard Jorgenson's Math class
first hour, but he did not come in for piano practice. I gave
him a few extra minutes before beginning to wonder where
he was. I went over to his room. He wasn't there and I had
a feeling that there was something odd about the room. His
mother's picture was gone from the dresser, that was it. I hoped
he had torn it up, but I felt sure he hadn't. I rushed over and
opened the closet door. None of his cowboy regalia was there.
He was apparently wearing his frontier pants, his cowboy
boots, and his pendleton shirt. These clothes were not permitted on school days. Kevin—I knew it—had decided he
couldn't face up to the Friday-night verdict of the faculty.
He had run away—and that was the worst crime a boy could
commit. Discovered, he was done for. A runaway is ruinous
to a school's reputation—for no one trusts a school that a
boy wants to leave—let alone that a boy can get away from
successfully. I had a frantic urgency to find Kevin before anyone else discovered he was gone. He couldn't be far because
he'd attended first class.

I needed help and, of course, there was no one so able to
give it as Joe, although Leonard or Roger or Marcus would
have been sympathetic with this situation. None of them,
however, would be willing to run the risk of Barrett's censure
as would Joe. He had a class—it was Third Form History and
it met, providentially, next door to Roger's Fifth Form History. I called Joe out to the corridor and explained.

"He can't be far," Joe consoled me. "In fact, I bet he's
hiding on the school grounds. He'd hardly dare just walk
away in broad daylight. He's probably waiting for night and
planning to swipe a horse. He's got sense enough to know he
couldn't get far on foot."

Just then Roger appeared at the doorway of his classroom.
"Did the little one fly the coop?"

"We don't know, Roger," I said.

"Joseph, you send your boys in to my class. I'm going to show some slides today—or I will, anyway, if I have your kids, too. You can say they joined up for that purpose. You going out to beat the bushes for the boy?"

"Yep—and thanks, Roger."

"But, Joe, what if Barrett should suddenly begin to wonder how Kevin's doing today?" I asked.

"Here's what you do, Peanut Cluster. You go to your room and for God's sake, you start in playing the 'Minuet in G.' It is always resounding through the halls at this hour. Barrett'll miss that—for a fact, he will. That's the sort of thing he notices. Play it. Start over and over—I'll find Kevin in an hour—trust me—you just play. Poor little punk, his record won't stand running away, so I've got to find him. He won't have a chance otherwise. So play on—cover for the little guy, will you?"

"But, of course, Joe—good luck—"

"Good luck," said Roger. "I'll move your class in with mine and explain to the Head about the film if he should show up."

I went up to my sitting room. I sat down at the piano and opened *Book Two, Simplified Classics for the Beginner*. I set the metronome, turned to page four, and began the "Minuet in G." Tra la—*la* la *la* la *la* la *la*—tra la *la*. "Begin again," I said to myself. Back I went. Tra la *la*—over and over— mistake after mistake—it was easy because my hands trembled. I was being Kevin Clark, practicing his music lesson, trying to get it "good" by Monday.

The "Minuet in G" became a "Danse Macabre" to me during the next hour. Every sound I heard in the hall frightened me. I was sure that any minute Barrett would burst in, or Munsey.

But finally the door opened and it was Joe. Beside him was

Kevin, somewhat disheveled, but properly dressed in school shorts and turtle-neck jersey. He looked like what he was— a little boy who had very recently thrown up and done an awful lot of crying.

"Start practicing, Kevin," said Joe, "and remember, you've been here all hour. I don't think anyone will ask you."

"And don't worry about mistakes, Kevin," I said.

"We'll forget mistakes, Kevin," said Joe.

Kevin took his seat at the piano, and none too soon. He had hardly begun when there was a knock on the door. It was Dr. Barrett. I felt as guilty as if I had an unpleasantly done-in body stuffed into my closet.

"Oh, hello," I said, nervously. "Come in!"

"How do you do?" He looked beyond me. "He *is* here. I thought he must be. I heard him practicing as usual, but Munsey thought he saw him in his boots and riding pants running out toward the stables at the end of first period."

"Munsey is a little unstrung, I would say," said Joe.

"Well, he *has* had quite a shock," agreed Barrett.

"Quite," said Joe.

Kevin played on—Tra la *la* la *la* la *la* la *la*—

I do not care for minuets—especially in G.

CHAPTER THIRTEEN

An Heir and a Parent

THERE was a time in my trusting youth when I believed that Heredity and Environment were simple subjects. Heredity I dismissed with a flick of the wrist as something of concern to peas only. I focused my faith on environment. I was conditioned to the democratic doctrine that genius didn't generate from genes. Every male child born in the United States could be president if he put his mind to it, and every girl could be a moving-picture star if she had the urge and the shape. Even the shape needn't be genetic since I had confidence in charm-school ads and believed that what God withheld Elizabeth Arden would provide. Basing my notions on heavy doses of Horatio Alger and Sunday school, I endorsed a log cabin or an urban tenement as optimum environment. Being poor, diligent, and God-fearing were all you needed to grow up to be a congressman or a steel tycoon.

Eventually, of course, I abandoned Alger as authority in favor of a required college reading list for Psychology I. My point of view shifted. There was, however, some rigidity in my altered concepts and a great deal of oversimplification. I felt, in my naïveté, that with all his marbles and a couple of undergraduate courses in psychology, any bird-brain could predict the personality potential of any child emerging from

131

a given environment. Being a well-qualified bird-brain myself, I was forever making such axiomatic predictions. Every
gesture I observed in a child was a foregone effect of some cause
and I'd label the causes and effects without hesitation.

I suppose I still subscribe to the basic reality of cause and
effect. I believe that the analyst who drapes a patient on the
couch for a couple of years can get a fair glimmer of what
makes him hate his mother and why he feels compelled to wash
his hands forty-seven times a day, etc. But the difference in
me is that now I leave all such speculation to the professionals
and I no longer toss personality appraisals off the top of my
head. I had not been at The Oaks very long before I realized
that any prognosticating I did was merely pig-in-poke pre-
diction. I discovered that I could not categorize my little boys
on the basis of anything—least of all heredity and environment. I'd no sooner get a boy in a pigeonhole than out he'd
fly.

The disgressing question crosses my mind at this point as
to whether even one of my Acorns ever turned out to be a
compulsive hand-washer. It seems unlikely. They all *loved*
dirty hands. In fact Bobby Lennox once voiced a rather
startling double-barreled ambition. "When I grow up," he
said, squinting his brows fiercely to emphasize his determination, "I'm never going to wear underwear and never ever
take baths."

As Joe said, "If Bobby achieves his ambition, he'll probably
spend his life in the stir on 'fragrancy' charges."

Bobby illustrates on a superficial level what prompted me
to quit my psychological shot-calling. Bobby came from a very
hygienic home and possessed admirably clean parents. His was,
in fact, an exceptionally good-smelling mother, who apparently not only bathed often but took no chances and also
doused herself in Chanel Number Five. She was a tidy dresser,
too, and a credit to Hattie Carnegie. And yet, Bobby's idea

of sartorial splendor was a dirty shirt with the collar turned up to tickle his ears. He always tied his cravat (decorated with abstractions done in yolk of egg) in such a way that one end of it hung down below his belt and the other just barely protruded beneath the knot at his neck. As an additional last-ditch defense against convention, Bobby lost shoelaces. Every Saturday, regularly, I bought him new ones—but he still preferred tying his little imported English bluchers with cotton cord or pinning them with saddle-blanket safety pins. Bobby owned a comb, but the only time I ever saw him use it willingly was the day he discovered that, wrapped in toilet paper, it made an excellent musical instrument. He is the only person I ever encountered in my life who looked forward eagerly to baldness.

In observing the startling dissimilarities between parents and children, I almost came to the conclusion that all the boys arrived in the world without benefit of biology.

Joe agreed with me. "Yep—the best parents have the worst children and the worst parents breed the seraphs. The social implications are terrifying, aren't they? Maybe they all just crawled up full-blown out of the alluvian slime, each one an individual fashioned according to his own whim and not beholden to ancestry."

There were exceptions, of course, to keep peace with the geneticists, if not the environmentalists. It was obvious that Homer had his father's brains and made excellent use of them. Larry Drummond's clear, direct, blue eyes were definitely a holdover from his father. And, of course, Kevin Clark, as his mother continually reminded him, got his unfortunate cowlick from his father, who ran off and left him absolutely nothing except three unmatched gold cuff links—and the cowlick. Also Peter Matthews III, had an aristocratic nose that had been in the family for generations. The Matthewses were always pointing to it proudly. "He has his grandfather's nose."

Even Peter accepted the genetics of his distinguished proboscis, but with a sense of humor that seemed most uninherent to the Matthews species. I remember he fell down once, and I called to him, "Did you hurt yourself, Peter?"

"Nope," he answered, "but I may have broken my grandfather's snozzle."

Another time, he remarked to Joe, "I sure hope this nose of my grandfather's doesn't get so old it dies before I do."

Joe said, "Well—I wouldn't worry. It can still run."

Apparently Peter's wit hadn't been in the family for three generations—or, if it had been, Peter had shown the enterprise and sensibility to overhaul and recondition it. Certainly, neither Gloria nor Peter II could possibly have thought up the remarks that Peter so facilely flipped off his tongue.

Peter was an anachronism in other areas, too. Carefully reared in an atmosphere that reeked of bigotry, he was, paradoxically, democratic almost to the point of defiance. He unerringly picked most "unsuitable" people to love. Me, for instance. Gloria, being quixotic, quickly revised the opinion of me which had shanghaied me into The Oaks.

Peter also doted on the school cook, a big economy-sized Spanish American named "Rosita." Rosita loved tequila not wisely but too well and could swear artistically in two languages—separately or blended. Rosita was only tolerated at The Oaks because children didn't ruffle her—not to violence anyway. Besides, no other cook, ruffled or unruffled, was willing to live in the country. Understandably, the boys were advised not to invade Rosita's domain. On several occasions, however, I found Peter installed on a stool in the kitchen, cheerfully helping Rosita shell peas, while he ate *tortillas* spread with mashed frijoles. Between bites, he burst into snatches of the "Versuviana," which Rosita was teaching him. "Put your little foot—put your little foot—" the huge woman and the small boy dueted happily. From time to time, Rosita pulled Peter off his perch and flung him through the gay dance that goes with the song. For Péter to tolerate Terpsichore was stark evidence of his devotion to Rosita, for Peter was one of dancing school's most rebellious victims.

Peter also adored Windy Bill Barkins, the school's horse wrangler, who divided his time between The Oaks and the Bar B Dude Ranch. Windy Bill was a "character" of considerably more picturesque appeal to a dude-ranch operator than a headmaster. Dr. Barrett was always trying to find a replacement for Windy Bill, but the old cowhand was so popular around the Prado Verde Valley that no self-respecting wrangler would have considered easing him out of his job so long as he wanted it. Windy Bill loved his job. Dr. Barrett was stuck with him.

He spit tobacco with an accuracy that was awesome, and he spoke a brand of English so cluttered with grammatical errors and colorful colloquialisms that it was almost incomprehensible. He loved all animals, including boys.

He told Peter once, "Iffin I had a young button of my own, I figger the right smartest thing I could do fer him would be to learn him to ride and rope any old highbindin' bushtail there ever was and fetch him up to be the best old horsesqueezin' waddy in the West."

Peter understood Windy Bill's language. "You could pretend I'm your button," Peter said, "because that's what I'm going to be, the best horsesqueezin' waddy in the West."

Windy Bill "fixed him up" a little lariat and started his training. Peter told his mother his career aspirations.

"But, darling," Gloria protested, "you want to be a fine gentleman like daddy, don't you, pet?"

"Nope," Peter said, "I think being a gentleman like daddy wouldn't be any fun. I would rather be a cowpoke or a bronc skinner. Jamie and me are both going to be waddies when we get big enough to be our own bosses."

Gloria immediately attributed these untraditional Matthews ambitions to Jamie's influence. Jamie was Peter's best
friend, and the Matthewses did not approve of the attach-
ment. Jamie's parents were very rich but, according to Gloria,
very common, having made their money by a mere fortuitous
accident of birth. This was how the Matthewses made theirs,
too—but the difference was in the nature of the Traverses'
accident.

Mr. Travers was born on, and inherited, a starvation farm
in Oklahoma which did not respond to the plow. However,
properly perforated, it produced seven lusty oil wells. The
Traverses, traditionally scramblers for pennies, suddenly had
so much money they didn't know what to do with it. (Their
efforts to solve this problem took some fairly bizarre forms.)
The Matthewses' money, on the other hand, was old. Like
Peter's nose, it had been in the family for generations. Gloria
explained it all to her own satisfaction, if not to mine: "Their
money is simply different from ours. New, you know." Personally, I have never found objectionable either freshly minted
coins or crisp greenbacks.

Gloria also always suspected Jamie of cultivating Peter in an
effort to pull himself up a couple of rungs on the social ladder.
Jamie's mother had her eye on the social ladder, I admit,
but Jamie didn't even know it existed. He and Peter were
just naturally thumb-and-finger. They loved each other. It
was as simple as that. They fought each other—and for each
other—like brothers.

No boy in the school, however, was quite so unexplainable
as Tim McNeill. Tim was Form Leader for the Pines. Dr.
Barrett often referred to him as "typical of our best achievement." Tim *was* a wonderful boy—but how and why and *who*
achieved him will forever remain a mystery to me. I am pretty
sure that his parents did not find him in the bulrushes. He
was beyond reasonable doubt the natural son of Mr. and Mrs.

J. Scott McNeill of Hollywood, New York, Miami, Santa Fe,
and many other parts, including Scandinavia. The McNeills,
singly and more rarely ensemble, were always in transit, so
they dropped in at the school more often than most parents.
Prado Verde was on the direct route to quite a few places.
Even my little Acorns—to whom Parents-were-Parents-and-so-
what!—tended to eye Mrs. McNeill with some startled wonder.

Mrs. McNeill was, it was widely rumored, a very smart
woman—smart in the head, that is, not chic. One encounter
with her, however, and I discounted such talk as malicious
gossip. There were a lot of things for which Mrs. McNeill
might have to answer, but no one, with even a modicum of
open-mindedness, could ever seriously blame a brain on her.
She was, I admit, a type that frequently arouses such suspicion.

She *did* things. Mostly she did things to the Arts. Sometimes she painted, canvases in gray and black that looked like
untidy piles of discarded army blankets but which were really
subtle intangibles like Despair and Gloom, caught in a rare
informal huddle. She had the unpleasant habit of giving her
paintings away. Most of the masters were unhappy victims of
her beneficence.

Sometimes she danced—barefoot. Sometimes she wrote
poetry—on a special typewriter ordered for the purpose and
deflowered of its capitals and punctuation keys. One of her
most memorable masterpieces always reminded me of a second-
grade spelling list:

> rain wind earth sky
> nature me
> moon sun stars sky
> nature me
> light dark
> nature me

Each morning she stepped onto her balcony in the nude
and prostrated herself three times to the sun. When it rained,

she bowed anyway—and took her routine cold shower direct from Nature's bounty. Like Jackie Cameron's mother, she ate sun-dried fruits, raw vegetables, and ground nuts (disguised as meatloaf) and she drank goat's milk in public and Old Bushmill in private.

She didn't condone personal adornment and wore clothes only as surrender terms to the *status quo*. In consequence, she looked a bit like a discouraged laundry bag with no hope of fulfillment. She scrupulously allowed all natural instincts full rein. She rode her own at a headlong gallop. By the same principle, she gave her husband a four-seasonal huntsman's license for his favorite sport—stalking flicker queens and other similar bright-plumed prey.

From her father she inherited the Bismo-Sodal Corporation, and with civilization increasing acidosis at a profitable rate, she was a power in her own right, without dependence on the movie industry which rewarded her husband lavishly in both money and ulcers.

Mr. McNeill hadn't always earned two hundred thousand per *annum*, however, and there had been a time when he could eat sauerkraut and onions pleasurably. It was during that regrettable period of misfortune twenty years before that he married Mrs. McNeill. He married her for her money, and she married him for breeding purposes. They were no longer interested in each other—their diverse purposes having been accomplished.

There is a population phenomenon in Southern California often referred to as the "lunatic fringe." The McNeills were not in this merely decorative category—they were the warp and woof of the cloth on which the fringe was strung. That they had in a connubial moment created Timothy was proof that Nature has a big sleeve up which to laugh.

Timothy at twelve was a solid citizen, unimaginative but thorough. No bypaths tempted him to wayward digression.

He walked the proper highroads with firm, purposeful tread. He was not compliant, however, and would stand as firmly with the minority as he would with the majority, according to which represented his principles. He was a peacemaker, but if a situation seemed to call for a fist, he folded his and used it.

He worked hard and made *A*'s. He played hard and made the football team. He sang on key. He used punctuation, according to the rules in the *Century Handbook*. When called upon to paint a picture, he painted exactly what he saw—all of it.

Marcus Carson, who taught Arts and Crafts, said, "You know, if Tim ever painted a golf course, everyone would be able to find his old balls because they'd sure as hell be in Tim's picture."

Everyone at The Oaks loved Tim—not for his human frailties, nor for his sparkling talents, for he had few of either. Everyone admired Tim because he was as dependable and predictable as the sun. He was kind and patient with everyone, particularly my little Acorns. He spent countless hours on the playfield practicing passing with them or teaching them to tackle. They put him on a pedestal, and they couldn't have picked a better boy for that notably shaky position.

We had one scholarship boy at The Oaks, Teddy Lane, but until I actually got all the boys identified I had Tim tagged as the student most probably deserving and needing scholarship aid. Except for being heir to a fortune, he was the perfect design for a small-town tradesman's son who would work his way through college and become the Mathematics teacher in his home-town high school and supervise the Boy Scouts on the side.

Tim was a biological sport. In a scientific study of environment—or heredity, either—Timothy would make a raving psychotic out of the sanest statistician. No allowance for probable error could account for Timothy. He was improbable error.

I saw a good deal more of Timothy than I did of most of the older boys because he voluntarily spent frequent evenings with the Acorns and me. I think he was unknowingly devising a substitute for the family life of which he had been deprived. Timothy and I became warm friends. He taught me to play chess and I taught him to dance backward. He was at the age where he was beginning to get a glimmer of the rewards of social dancing. He danced intently with his tongue stuck out between tight lips, much in the same manner a younger boy tackles an arithmetic problem. He kept time by shaking his head slightly in rhythm to the music. He promised to be a reliable, if not inspired, dancer.

"But yeeps!" he said to me, "I don't see how anyone ever gets so he can go backward. I keep bumping into people all the time. The boys think it is very funny to bump, but I expect when you grow up you have to go backward sometimes and it's better not to bump."

Night after night between the Acorns' bedtime and Tim's, he and I practiced this complication. We were not permitted to play a phonograph or the radio after eight, so we sang over and over: "I Can't Give You Anything but Love, Baby" and "Oh, We Ain't Got a Barrel of Money." These were, ironically enough, Tim's favorite songs.

Between dances we talked. He confided his ambitions— both long-term and immediate goals. He aspired to a future in the Forest Service.

"I figure," he told me seriously, "I might be able to get a job to start with on a trail crew or as a fire guard and then work up." He saw himself rising to supervisor of the Coconino and then the Kaibab Forest and eventually regional director in Albuquerque.

"I think I would like to marry Larry Drummond's sister, Christine. It's funny about girls, isn't it?"

"They're somewhat bewildering, you mean?"

"Well—it's sort of queer about girls. I hated girls last year. This year I like girls, especially Christine. She says my haircut is sharp and she thinks I dance okay. I think she's pretty."

"Did you tell her so?"

"Well—I didn't want her to think I was silly or anything so I just said that one thing was for sure, she'd never have to worry about being ugly."

"That was a clever way of putting it," I said. "Quite subtle."

"You think so? Funniest thing, though, is the way I felt inside me. I don't quite know what to say to describe it. It was sort of terribly glad—gurgly, if you know what I mean." Tim hesitated, and the color rose in his cheeks. "You know what, I wanted to kiss her. Sort of crazy, suddenly wanting to kiss a girl. Andy Mansfield has kissed *nine* girls. Of course, the reason I decided I'd like to marry Christine is because she used to live in a Mexican mining camp."

"Oh?" I raised my voice gently.

"Yeh, before Larry and Christine came to Arizona to go to boarding schools, that's where they lived. She'd make a good wife for a ranger because of that, I figure."

He went on to tell me he planned on six children. He visualized all six of them and Christine waiting behind a white picket fence for him when he came home after a hard day's work.

"Christine would get to be a good cook, and after dinner I'd help her with the dishes and we'd fool around with the kids and put them to bed and then we'd play chess and talk and dance, too, maybe— Say, we better practice it backward some more."

Where Timothy ever got the wings for such flights of fantasy about family life, I shall never know. He didn't even

learn chess from his father. He figured out the game by reading the *Encyclopaedia Britannica's* description of it. Maybe he
also dug into "The Mores of Middle Class Home Life" in the
Britannica and found it good.

His more immediate goal the first year I was at The Oaks
was to earn enough money to buy Cord Logan's old roping
saddle. Cord Logan was a cowboy at the Bar B Dude outfit.
He had a hand-tooled saddle for sale that appealed to Tim.
"I could use that saddle the rest of my life," Tim explained
to me. "It would be a good trail saddle when I'm a forest
ranger."

Allowances at The Oaks were established by regulation and
no boy was permitted extra pocket money from home. No
one ever had enough cash in hand for sporty spending. However, for Tim to get the saddle was a simple process. All he
needed to do was write his mother or father and say he wanted
it—or, even easier, go to Dr. Barrett and name his whim. The
purchase price would have been promptly forthcoming from
Tim's deposited drawing account for extras. All the boys had
such accounts to cover clothing replacements, tutoring, music
lessons, equipment, books, etc.

But Tim, with his implausible instincts, decided to earn
the money for the saddle. Traditional boyhood jobs are not
plentiful in a school setting. No paper routes are available
and the lawns are shorn by professionals. We all recognized
the merit in Tim's determination, however, and provided
whatever profitable tasks we could for him. The Jorgensons
hired him to fill the wood closet in their cottage every week.
Joe and Dr. Barrett paid him to wash their cars and Windy
Bill gave him a dollar every Saturday for helping to clean out
the stables. He shined shoes for some of his less energetic
friends at the rate of five cents a pair, guaranteeing them pass-
able for Sunday-morning inspection. In addition, persuaded
by an ad in *Boy's Life* that lauded the fortune to be picked up

by any enterprising young man willing to invest $2.25 in seed packets, he developed a garden-seed business. Of course, this necessitated selling his schoolmates on gardening. His leadership made this easy. Almost every boy in the school planted a row of carrots or beets or radishes, having purchased ten cents' worth of seeds from Tim. Tim was so grateful for their business, he helped most of them plant, and eventually cultivate and irrigate.

Joe was so afraid that Cord Logan would get another buyer for the saddle before Tim accumulated the purchase price that he went over to put down a ten-dollar option on it out of his own pocket. Cord, however, was swayed by Windy Bill into an enthusiasm for Tim's project almost as great as Joe's own. He agreed, of course, to hold the saddle without token.

Most boys bog down on such prolonged ventures, but weeks went by and Tim continued to pursue his dedicated purpose. Tim's project began to take on meaning for all the boys. Nobody asked the question any more, "Why don't you see if you can touch your old man for the saddle?"

Instead, the daily query was, "How much you got saved up now, Tim?"

He had twenty-two dollars at the time his father and mother stopped by on their way to Santa Fe. The saddle was almost his. Cord Logan had become so sympathetic about the long-term deal that he had offered to cut his original quotation of thirty dollars to twenty-five, if Tim cinched the transaction by the first of May. "I hanker to get shed of the saddle before summer," he explained to Tim to justify his generosity. He did want to sell it, but obviously not badly enough to accept either of the two forty-dollar offers that had been made by departing guests from the Bar B.

I do not blame Dr. Barrett for mentioning Tim's venture to his parents. Dr. Barrett from start to finish regarded the project as praiseworthy. He was plainly and simply proud of

Tim, and so he passed on the story of the coveted saddle to the McNeills, expecting sympathetic response. Dr. Barrett was an expert and usually got what he expected from parents, but he came a cropper this time. Dr. Barrett, Joe, Roger, and I were all having sherry with the McNeills in the headmaster's study.

"Why didn't the kid ask *me* for the saddle?" Mr. McNeill wanted to know.

"Don't you see, it meant something special to him to earn it," Dr. Barrett explained, and stood his ground. "I think it was admirable of him."

"But, goodness!" Mrs. McNeill put in. "Isn't it rather over-emphasizing material things for Tim to care so much for a hand-tooled saddle? Frankly, Dr. Barrett, I think your encouragement of this fiasco is unhealthy. Now, Tim doesn't get this from me." Her frown was an accusing finger pointed at Mr. McNeill. "*I* believe in the simplicities. I'd like to see Tim mount a barebacked Palomino and ride in the wind and feel one with both the animal and the elements. It is the same sort of thing that makes me dance barefoot. I touch Nature."

"Oh, lay off Nature, Millicent," Mr. McNeill said sharply. "I, for one, wish you'd keep your shoes on. There's nothing wrong with a kid wanting a classy saddle. I suppose the other kids have them?"

"No—no," Dr. Barrett went on, almost impatiently. "It isn't that. Some of them have special saddles—yes—but it isn't the saddle itself in this case. It's what earning the saddle apparently symbolizes to Timothy."

Joe and I exchanged awed glances. Barrett was turning into one of our teammates!

"Sounds like a bunch of crap to me," Mr. McNeill said.

"Did you ever want something very badly when you were a boy?" Dr. Barrett asked him.

"Yes, plenty of times, but I wasn't such a damned nincompoop that I would have cleaned out stables to get it if my dad were standing over me with an open wallet. I worked when I was a kid, but because I *had* to. I made up my mind no son of mine would ever have to slug it out the way I did."

There seemingly was no indoctrinating Mr. McNeill. Dr. Barrett recognized his defeat. "I would much rather you didn't mention any of this to Tim," he suggested firmly.

"Don't worry, I wouldn't know what to say to him," Mr. McNeill agreed carelessly. "I don't understand that kid."

The McNeills finally left and we all breathed easier.

"Say, Barrett," Joe spoke for all of us. "You handled that very well. I think you and I might understand each other if we put our minds to it."

"Possibly," said Barrett curtly. Then, with a light touch of almost Hargrave humor, he added, "if we had that kind of time on our hands." I detected a fleeting but pleased expression on his face. Even Barrett, I thought, accepted as accolade Joe's approval.

Five more days would see Tim's saddle deal consummated. He had Joe's car to wash, his regular stable job with Windy Bill, and his weekly fare for the wood box. His total would certainly reach twenty-five by Saturday. He had lined up the order in which the boys were to take turns trying the saddle.

However, his father apparently stopped somewhere along the highway to Santa Fe and made a telephone call to Phoenix. Midweek, following the McNeills' visit, a huge carton was delivered by special trucking service to Tim. Tim was batting some flies for the Acorns on the front lawn when the box arrived. They all dropped their mitts and balls to gather around while Tim unwrapped the bulky contents. Packages were always exciting. Sometimes they contained sharable food. Unfortunately, there was no cake in Tim's parcel.

It was a brand-new, custom-made, full-stamp saddle, lavish

in silver mounting. Porter's in Phoenix had sent it up on special order. "That saddle would make a 'Hi-ho, Silver' out of any old cutback," Joe said later. It was gear designed to lead a parade, to charm an MGM property man, to delight the heart of a boy. It brought no outburst, however.

"It's a *saddle?*" Bewildered, Jamie almost whispered the words.

"Yes," said Tim. "It's a saddle. I guess there's been some mistake. It's meant for somebody else." Frantically, he looked around the sober-faced crowd for reassurance. "It must belong to someone else," he repeated louder. The boys lowered their eyes and fell silent. Larry Drummond kicked at the grass and Bobby Lennox plucked at the buckle on his catcher's mitt.

"Tim, it's got your name on it, Tim," Peter finally said. He pointed to the saddle seat where the uncontroversial identity was displayed in the hand-tooled lettering: TIMOTHY MC-NEILL. "I betcha, though, it's for some other guy named 'Timothy McNeill,' because—because everybody calls *you* Tim," Peter hastily added as if guilt-ridden for his revelation.

"I betcha," echoed Jamie.

"No, it's for me," said Tim quietly. "My father sent it. There's a card here, see. Says, 'Buy yourself a necktie with your money. Here's a saddle from your Dad.' "

"It's a *swell* saddle, Tim. It's a super saddle," said Peter.

"Yeh, it's *super*," several voices reiterated the sentiment, but no one said it was better than Cord Logan's saddle—which it was. No one ever mentioned Cord Logan's saddle again, so far as I know. Except Timothy. He called Cord that night at the Bar B, and asked him if there was anyone else who might buy the saddle. Tim was fair through it all. He didn't want Cord to be caught with unsalable merchandise, with most of his best prospects, the winter visitors, already headed home.

"I won't need the saddle, Cord," he said, "but I expect you

kept it for me, so I feel I should pay you what I've saved up so far anyway. I've got nothing to spend the money on."

Cord, of course, would not accept such largess. As a matter of fact, he sold the saddle the next day for forty dollars instead of the twenty-five he'd asked Tim.

Tim's new saddle was beautiful. Windy Bill placed it on a saddle rack in the barn. He did not spit tobacco on it, but he had it so located that he just barely grazed the horn every time he aimed for the barn door. The saddle was never ridden by Tim or anyone else. No boy at The Oaks could possibly have defined intellectually what that saddle represented, but emotionally they all felt its impact.

It was shortly after this that Tim gave up horseback riding. Since he decided not to be a forest ranger, after all, he concluded he might as well concentrate on his tennis instead. He wrote and asked his father for a new racquet.

He did not speak very fully or freely to me of the saddle. All he said was, "It's a beautiful saddle. It is—it is—but— why did he ever do it? Why *did* he?"

CHAPTER FOURTEEN

The Light Fantastic

Iᴛ was amazing to me how frequently the boys needed new clothes. They always arrived in September with lavish wardrobes and when they returned after Christmas holidays they were loaded with replenishments. And yet, dancing school or any other important event always revealed the fact that few of them had proper apparel for the occasion. Boys and haberdashery are notoriously uncongenial. Still—this was not just a wear-and-tear phenomenon, for there were some very curious exceptions. Teddy Lane, Larry Drummond, and Roland Webster, among boarders, and Homer Curtis and Sandy Spencer, day boys, always seemed to have well-fitting, suitable trappings on tap. Oddly paradoxical, too, these particular boys were from the more modest homes and came to school relatively light on luggage. It did not follow that they were more careful with clothing.

I finally recognized the obvious. Rich boys outgrow their clothes faster than poor boys. I cast this morsel at a socially serviceable friend of mine once and she rose to the bait.

"You see," she said, setting her lips into a thin line of disapproval, "that just goes to show that rich children have superior nutrition and have a better chance to realize their physical potential."

"No," I said smugly. "You social scientists tend to leap over logic to false conclusions. You don't have to have a million dollars to provide vitamins. It's simple—and not at all tragic. Rich boys outgrow their clothes faster than poor boys because their clothes fit them properly at time of purchase."

That's all there was to it. By Christmastime, Teddy Lane's twenty-dollar suit, selected realistically to accommodate growth, looked like a Brooks Brothers triumph compared to Peter Matthews's fifty-dollar, imported English flannel which was bursting at the seams.

With the onset of dancing school two weeks away, there was a sudden flurry of interest in clothes. There was much measuring of the discouraging stretch of bare leg between shorts and socks and the exposure of arm between cuff and wrist. As a consequence, I had a long list of important commissions for my shopping trip to Phoenix. I also had a long list of volunteers who generously offered to go along to "help me." You know—protect me from holdups on the highway and assist me in getting tickets for the movies when I got tired of shopping, and escort me to the rodeo in the event I decided I wanted to go, and guard me from drowning in the Arizona-Biltmore swimming pool where they figured any fool would certainly spend part of his day in Phoenix. Incidentally, they were willing, of course, to squander five or ten minutes in Goldwater's and Porter's helping me select the mere fifty or sixty assorted items—shoes, ties, trousers, etc.—demanded by dancing school.

As usual, however, on such expeditions, the basis of selection of traveling companions was not the willingness or congeniality of volunteers, but expediency. On my rare trips to Phoenix, I filled the station wagon with boys who had to see the orthodontist. Malocclusion became a coveted condition. It got you places.

I remember one day I had six varied-sized boys with me

at luncheon in the Westward Ho Dining Room. A loud-whispering matron at a nearby table was expressing to her companion her startled wonder at the size of my family.

"Imagine it! Six—all boys, and so near the same age. She looks quite young, too."

"The children don't resemble each other much," remarked her companion. "Maybe they aren't all hers."

"Obviously they're hers," the stubborn matron insisted. "They're too relaxed and behave too badly for guests. Besides, see, they all have braces. Their father must have terrible teeth."

No boy would have admitted he was in favor of dancing school, but no boy could, without delicate perjury, have proved he was actively against it. My Acorns were fated to trip the gay fantastic for the first time, and they were violently verbalizing their protests. My shopping list, however, betrayed a subtle but unmistakable overtone of enthusiasm. Almost every boy sentenced to the "Ordeal" had slipped up to me and whispered his wishes, thinly disguised as emergency needs.

Even Peter, probably the waltz's most ardent antagonist, made his apologetic request for refurbishment. "I think my shoes are too short and I might get blisters if I dance in them," he told me. "It's bad enough having to push those girl babies around, without blisters, too. I think I better have new shoes. I saw some simply super black-and-white ones that have sort of air holes all over them. I'd like that kind. They'd be good if my feet got hot."

Our dancing school was a cooperative venture with the Shadow Creek School for Girls, located twenty miles away. We drove our boys over in the school station wagons once a week. Andy Mansfield started calling the students at Shadow Creek "girl babies." My little Acorns always imitated the speech of the Junipers, who imitated the speech of the Spruces, who imitated the speech of the Pines. So everyone used the term "girl babies"—we all spoke the same language. Colorful slang phrases ran their course through the school like epidemic rashes. We did, of course, inoculate the boys against a few more dangerously contagious words.

"Someone must have come to my room and tore up every single tie I own," Jeffrey complained to me. "I just guess I will have to get a new tie for this awful dancing school. I was thinking maybe a red one with yellow birds on it might be okay. Cord Logan's got one like that and his is swell because it hooks in back and you never even have to tie it. You think that would be good, sir?"

I assured Jeffrey that I thought yellow birds on red would be utterly seductive, especially in a natty ready-tied job. When I came to The Oaks, I made the mistake of suggesting appropriate clothing and harmonious color combinations to the boys. I assumed that becoming propriety in dress would give them social ease. This was unsound reasoning. I discovered that whatever struck the fancy of a little boy supported him socially, irrespective of its suitability to either himself or the situation. I became as permissive about clothing as the school rules allowed. My efforts at guidance were limited pretty much to insistence on at least Grade B cleanliness and dissuasion from appearing in something that might distress Dr. Barrett to the point of open disapproval. Also, I manipulated enough to discourage any costume that might possibly be target for the barbarous ridicule of the older boys.

My theory was that just as a four-year-old drifts away from his enthusiasm for a portrait of Mickey Mouse on his pajamas, an eight-year-old eventually abandons his jewel-studded cowboy belt with two holsters and two guns. After all, by the age of twelve, most boys no longer encounter perils that require quick drawing of cap pistols.

Dr. Barrett did not share this point of view. He believed that the only way boys learned what to wear and when was by a set of well-defined, forceful instructions. He seemed to think that if a boy were permitted to don a leather aviator's helmet and goggles when he had no intention of piloting an airplane, he would be permanently conditioned, and until the day he tottered to his grave he would wear inappropriate headgear.

Dr. Barrett was wrong. I ran into Bobby Lennox a couple of years ago in New York. He was not wearing a miner's cap, equipped with a headlight—his favorite top-dressing when I knew him best. As a matter of fact, he was wearing a Homburg. Bobby managed to achieve the miner's cap through some very expensive barter with Larry Drummond, who got it from a mucker who worked for his father. Bobby gave Larry a pair of cowboy boots, three extremely talented "laggers," and a sun-dried tibia, enhanced as a collector's item by the unsubstantiated fable that it was once an articulating part of a live Indian. Rosita insisted the bone was tossed out with the garbage following a leg-of-lamb dinner, but the boys merely scoffed at Rosita's credentials as an anthropologist. The treasure remained a remnant of an Apache—a fierce one, at that, named "Wom-pooh-pooh."

In spite of Larry's take of treasures, the cap still constituted a bargain for Bobby. He never did a bit of mining, but topped with the bizarre headgear, he felt as secure as a crowned prince. I even toyed with the whimsy of allowing him to wear it during Reading Class, his hardest subject, in which his sense of inadequacy always tangled his tongue.

Of course, our dancing-school regimentals were pretty well standardized—white-flannel slacks or shorts and the school blazers, gray flannel, trimmed in green with the form insignia on the pockets. Jeffrey's red-and-yellow cravat would not enhance this basic costume. However, if Jeffrey thought a red tie with yellow birds was dashing, it would make him feel dashing. If Peter thought ventilated shoes would make the fox trot tolerable, I'd comb every store in Phoenix for the coveted clothes.

Jamie had his problem, too. Jamie always scratched when he wore wool. Consequently, his wardrobe was lavish in linen and cotton gabardine. However, white flannels were definitely the posh gentleman's choice for dancing school.

"Look, kid," Andy Mansfield told Jamie, looking down from his lofty tower of experience, "you just can't go around scratching yourself the way you do in front of all those girl babies. Besides, you need both your hands for dancing."

"What do I have to do with my hands?" asked Jamie ignoring that part of the problem which involved mere social nicety.

"Dope! You have to hold onto the girl with your hands."

"Oh, yeeps!" Jamie scowled. "Did you hear that, Pete? I never even thought about the fact that you got to touch the girl babies, did you, huh, Pete?"

"Sure, I knew it all the time," Peter said, and shrugged his shoulders.

Jamie came to me with a proposal. "Now, lookit," he began, "I don't care what those dumb girl babies like, see? But the kids all say they won't dance with you unless you got flannel pants. My mother says I have to learn to dance so I guess I'm going to just simply *have* to get some flannel pants."

"You could wear your white linen ones," I suggested. "They are very nice. You aren't very comfortable in wool, you know, Jamie."

"Yeh—and don't think I care what I wear, but I figure I better have the flannels. I want long ones, too. I'm too old for short pants now. I'm almost nine, you know. I was talking to Windy Bill about it—and you know what? He wears long underwear under his frontier pants 'cause they itch him

same as pants itch me. Maybe you could get me some long
underdrawers when you go to Phoenix. And the pants, of
course."

Soberly I added the items to my list. Phoenix, however,
where the temperature is likely to hover in the high nineties
had no long drawers on sale anywhere. I got the flannels, however, and Jamie solved his lingerie problem by wearing light-
weight cotton pajamas under his pants in lieu of longies.

"I don't want any old white-flannel pants." Winthrop
played it subtle. "I suppose I have to have some, though,
huh?"

"Yes, you certainly do!" My answers to such questions were
always firm, even argumentative in tone. "And don't you
make any fuss about it either!" I obligingly bolstered the
myth that they were all being persecuted into grooming themselves. Dressing for a party is one process in which men like
to have women push them around. They want to look like
dazzling cavaliers, but they much prefer to pretend that the
effect was achieved by mere accident or as a result of com-
plying with the whim of a foolish woman.

Boarding-school boys have a few advantages over home-
grown children when it comes to dancing school. They march
into the fray, not as lone knights but as a battalion. They have
the support of other tyros like themselves, and in addition,
they are backed up by veterans of one, two, and even three
seasons of dancing. They are also providentially spared the
gallery of tense mothers, with their contagious anxiety.

Andy Mansfield, age thirteen, had the most campaign rib-
bons—and more incidental decorations also. He was very wise
in both the customs of dancing school and the habits and
mores of girl babies. He had not only worked through the
tango, he'd even worked through his misogyny. He liked girls
and was already sophisticated enough to admit it.

He and Tim and some of the others, mellow with their

years of living, shared their sophisticated knowledge with their callow schoolmates about to make their first *Putsch*. It was at such times that I was reminded that, although my Acorns were very young, so also were all the "older" boys at The Oaks.

Actually, we had only one aged gentleman on our roster. Homer, who had survived the ripe old age of nine, and was well on his way to ten, was pretty world-weary. He was to meet the challenge of dancing school along with the boarders. His attitude was one of blasé acceptance. "Dancing," he announced, "dates back to the primitive. Ever since the days of the savage aborigine, human beings have expressed themselves in rhythm, first to the tom-tom beat and later to more complicated music. For the most part, such dancing stemmed from religious ritual, but eventually it became a sexual manifestation."

The Acorns snorted, but the older boys pricked up their ears. Occasionally Homer gave with information that was a bit hard come by in their environment.

"Dancing became a part of courtship," Homer continued his lecture. "It will not interest most of us at present, but eventually we will find dancing useful. When we are at the mating age."

"Whee—" gasped Andy, disappointed at the paucity of the revelations but impressed at Homer's erudition. "Get a load of that kid, won't you?"

"Don't pay any attention to Homer," Tim cautioned. "After all, kids, he's never been to dancing school. It's really fun, once you get the hang of it."

"I've never been to the penitentiary either," countered Homer, "but I know it has barred windows. It's the state of your glands, Tim," continued Homer with authority, "that makes you enjoy dancing. If you were Polynesian, you'd be at the mating age, you know. You're pubescent."

"You better dry up, Homer," said Tim. "You talk too big for your size."

"Yeh—you sure do," said Bobby. "You won't even be able to dance worth anything, Homer. You can't even play football as good as Kevin even."

"I shall dance satisfactorily," said Homer, "because dancing has more point than football. Therefore, I shall be more strongly motivated."

"Oh, freeze, Homer," said Andy. "I'll tell you kids what's what. Most *important*—when you pick someone to dance with, pick the little kids. You can imagine how I'd feel dancing with a nine-year-old girl baby and think how silly you'd look dancing with an older dame of, say, twelve. It's silly and it's always happening because you little twirps don't pay any attention to how old the girls are. You just ask the first one you run into to dance. They can't refuse—it's the rule—and Miss Pettigrew makes everyone dance—that's the rule, too—so us older men have to drag the leftover little girl babies around. It's awful."

"Should we ask them how old they are before we tell them we want to dance?" demanded Kevin soberly.

"*Honestly!*" sighed Andy. "Of course not." Then he giggled. "Just pick the ones that are real flat above the waist." Andy was feeling his age.

"Don't say things like that, Andy," Tim reproved. "Just pick the real short ones, kids, and the ones in short dresses. That's the best way to tell if they're under twelve. They let them wear longer dresses when they're twelve. You kids just lay off the long dresses—see?"

"But some of *us* got long pants now," Bobby said.

"Oh, honestly!" said Andy. "What kind of pants you have has nothing whatsoever to do with it."

"And don't act silly," advised Tim. "There's too much

horsing around. Some of the older boys do it, too. Don't horse
around."

The Acorns all looked very solemn and nodded sagely as if
Tim's advice had sounded the depths of their souls. However,
telling a bunch of little boys not to horse around at dancing
school is like telling a bunch of horses not to horse around
in a pasture. It was excellent advice, of course, but quite
against Nature.

"It sure doesn't sound like much fun," said Peter.

"There's food—Cokes and cake usually, and ice cream,"
Tim said.

"Oh, that's different," said Bobby. "Do you get much?" He
sounded like a borderline starvation case.

"Practically all you want," encouraged Tim.

"Gee, that's different, isn't it different, Pete?" said Jamie.

"Yeh—that's different and we can stay up till ten-thirty,
too. That's also different," said Peter.

"You'll just get sleepy," said Homer cynically.

"Maybe you'll get sleepy, Homer," said Bobby, "but I never
ever get sleepy. I wouldn't even sleep nights if it weren't the
law."

Children must, I suppose, be taught to dance. But sometimes I think some enterprising scholar ought to add a test
to the big battery of psychological tests entitled, "Dancing
Readiness," similar to the "Reading Readiness" test. Most
of my little Acorns were not ready to dance. They were ready
to chase each other around the dance floor, however—play
tag, hit each other, and make what they regarded as very
"funny faces" and "funny noises."

Miss Pettigrew, the dancing teacher, had many years of
coping behind her. Perhaps too many. She was always in step
with the music, but I always felt she was a little out of step

with the times. She had three quieting devices—her voice, her
hands which she would clap like a professional applauder,
and a whistle which she carried around her neck on a chain,
like a basketball coach. The whistle was purely for emergencies.

Miss Pettigrew lined the boys up on one side of the room
and the girls on the other. At the start, Miss Pettigrew gave
all the new dancers exclusive use of their own feet. Beginners
danced alone until later in the evening when they were given
partners to torment. The boys and girls who had previous
instruction were permitted to dance together during this preliminary period.

Miss Pettigrew's high-pitched voice rose above the blatant
rhythms of the piano, beating the Strauss out of the "Blue
Danube." "Step—step—slide," she shrieked. "Young people,
step—step—slide." And down the center of the room Miss
Pettigrew stepped, stepped, and slid, and on each side of the
room the two columns of small boys and girls stepped, stepped,
and slid in imitation. There is a facial contortion common
among beginning fandangoists that, for want of a better term,
I have always called the "Dismal Dancer's Expression." It is
compounded of sober effort, belligerency, and the awful reali-
zation that the poor victim is making a silly fool of himself.
Most of my Acorns directed this triple-threat scowl at their
feet. They watched their feet constantly, as if what were
going on was completely autonomous, undictated by their
brains. Every now and then Miss Pettigrew, in rhythm to the
music, would throw in a little advice. "Young people—step—
step—slide—one—two—three—don't—watch—feet—one—
two—three." Guiltily every child lifted his eyes. Left un-
guarded, most of the feet immediately did unorthodox things.

Miss Pettigrew believed in infusing into the education of
the feet education in the amenities as well. During the brief
respites from "step—step—slide," the boys were required to

repeat again and again the request for the dance. They had to select a girl, walk across the room to her, bow from the waist, and then say, "May I have this dance?" or "Are you engaged?"

This latter approach sent the twelve-year-olds into great bursts of hilarity. "Are you engaged?" the boys asked, and invariably came the giggled answer, "No, but I'm married." This was the height of wit and, no matter how often it was repeated, it sent everyone into paroxysms of laughter.

Miss Pettigrew also insisted that the children practice what she called "polite conversation." "Tell each other about your interests and ask questions to bring out your partner's interests. This is as much a part of dancing, young people, as learning the steps."

My little Acorns tried, of course. The boys always "try" the first night at dancing school. However, with the exception of Homer, they sounded like a bunch of census takers. Homer got a little blue-eyed girl under his spell and firmly informed her of his interests.

"I shall tell you of my interests," he said. "My interests cover many areas, but at the present time I am particularly concerned with the practical and theoretical aspects of projectile warfare. Do you have interests, and if so, what are they?"

Looking a bit frightened, the little girl confided in Homer that she was quite interested in paper dolls and that she liked the "Bobbsey Twin" series very much.

"You are obviously not the intellectual type," said Homer. "Frankly, I am too young to have any biological interest in you. We have very little in common. However, since this is merely an artificial situation created for training purposes anyway, you can go ahead and tell me about the Bobbsey Twins if you want to. I might as well learn to be a good listener."

Most of the other little boys hammered away at the vital statistics.

"How old are you?" asked Jamie.

"I am nine," answered a polite little girl named Barbara. "How old are you?"

Jamie apparently was concentrating so hard on remembering the questions he had thought up to draw out Barbara that he brooked no cross-examination. He left all Barbara's questions dangling.

"How many brothers and sisters do you have?" he demanded.

"I have one brother," said Barbara. "How many brothers and sisters do you have?"

"Where do you live?" answered Jamie.

"I live in San Francisco. Where do *you* live?"

"What grade are you in?" asked Jamie—and so the interview went its lopsided way.

The only truly animated conversation I observed was between Peter and a little girl named Jennifer Kennedy. Jennifer had her face in a frown and her underlip protruded. She wore a white-organdy party dress with a pink sash, but it was not her type. She looked like a pigtailed pugilist. Peter's scowl matched hers in severity. I drifted in their direction with the frank purpose of eavesdropping.

"We think you kids are a bunch of stinkers," I heard Jennifer say.

"We think the same of you. We wouldn't even be here if it weren't the law," said Peter. "We all hate women."

"We hate boys, too. I could get you down if I wanted to," announced Jennifer.

"You could not," said Peter. "No girl can get me down—not that I'd bother to knock down a girl. Too much trouble. I wouldn't want to get my hands dirty."

As I strolled by, I noticed Jennifer roll her eyes at Peter

in a conspiratorial manner. "Sh—" she managed to warn him, and then her voice changed into one of charming social grace. "Do you like chocolate sauce or butterscotch better, Peter?" she asked quickly.

"Chocolate," Peter answered. "Which do you like?"

Apparently Jennifer regarded me as out of earshot. "If I had a whole pitcherful of chocolate sauce I'd pour it right on you."

"If I had some butterscotch, I'd rub it in your hair," Peter countered.

"Wouldn't that be *simply* awful?" said Jennifer, and giggled.

Suddenly they both laughed, and then Peter said, "Gee, I wish we could go outside and run just as fast as we can and see who can run fastest. I bet I could beat you."

"Well—maybe *you* could, but nobody else could. You look awful strong." Love in bloom. "But we can't go outside," said Jennifer soberly, shaking her head. "We are not allowed *ever* to go outside. That's what the older girls told us. Do not dance with anyone over eleven and do not go outside—ever. They said those were the most important things to remember."

Jennifer was certainly right about "going outside." Miss Pettigrew always opened her lecture on the rewards of social dancing by speaking a few modestly veiled words on the pitfalls of the dance, "going outside" being the most treacherous. She invested the night air with mysterious, evil dangers. "Going outside" in any company whatsoever—or even alone—implied moral turpitude at its most turpid. If a boy strolled out alone, he was being uncooperative. If he strolled out in the company of another boy, he was cooperating in uncooperativeness. If he went outside with a girl, he was, of course, suspected of "cooperating."

Miss Pettigrew learned in time, to her verbalized distress, on which boys she should put the watchful eye. But that first

evening she ignored Andy Mansfield, since certainly his dancing needed less attention than any of the other boys'.

Andy took Marybelle Kirkwood "outside." He was unob-
served by Miss Pettigrew, and wouldn't have been discovered
at all except that he made a fatal tactical error. The next dance,
he slipped "outside" again with another thirteen-year-old,
Penelope Patterson. Marybelle Kirkwood witnessed this fickle
duplicity and apparently did not endorse it. She called the
matter to Miss Pettigrew's attention very subtly.

"I wonder," she remarked casually, "for goodness' sake,
where Andy and Penny are, Miss Pettigrew. I have been
looking for Penny to tell her something."

This started Miss Pettigrew wondering, too. She promptly
herded the wayward ones back in. "What were you two doing
outside?" she demanded. Her outraged voice implied that
the culprits were all but billeted for reform school.

"Why, nothing. Just cooling off," said Penelope.

"That's a lie!" protested Marybelle. "You were kissing
Andy."

"Why, whatever gave you such a silly idea?" asked Penelope
who was somewhat advanced for her years.

"I know because Andy took me outside last dance and
kissed me." I suppose her confession was a combination of
feminine pride—Andy was regarded as a dizzy attainment—
and a clumsy effort to prove her accusation.

"Oh my! *Marybelle!*" gasped Miss Pettigrew.

"Well—really, Belly," said Penelope, "just because you are
that type girl is no reason I am. Andy didn't even try to kiss
me because he respects me, don't you, Andy?"

"That's right," agreed Andy piously. "I sure do." He was
not very subtle but he did recognize a reprieve when he saw
one.

Miss Pettigrew was very distressed about the whole unfortunate affair. "My young people just don't do this sort of

thing," she said. She sent Marybelle to her room and made Andy sit on the sidelines for the rest of the evening. She merely told the "respected" Penelope that she must remember the rules better next time. Whenever Penelope danced by the bench-warming Andy, she fluttered her eyes at him and he ogled back.

Andy never admitted that he didn't "respect" Penelope too much to kiss her. However, he was in my station-wagon load on the way home, and bragged to the boys that he had kissed eleven girls. Since he had been bragging on the way over that he had kissed *nine* girls, I imagine that Penelope, too, had become a statistic.

"Why do you kiss girls?" demanded Peter.

"To see what it's like," said Andy.

"But I should think you'd see what it's like after you did it once. Why did you have to kiss *eleven* girls?" asked Peter.

"It's different every time," announced Andy.

"Aw—baloney—" scoffed Peter. "I been kissed by my mother, my aunt Martha, my aunt Carol, and by my cousin Pamela, and I guess when I was very young I was kissed by a couple of other dames. I didn't know any better. And the whole mess of them just kiss the same, except in different spots on my face."

"I do not want to kiss any girls." Jamie supported Peter. "Of course, I'll kiss my mother because it's a habit with her, but I sure hate that lipstick all over me. And when I get married I'll kiss my wife, I suppose, when I go to the office. They make you do it. Only I probably won't get married."

"When I get married I'm going to get a divorce right away," Bobby said. "My dad is going to get one."

"I like Christine best," Tim announced dreamily to no one in particular.

"I liked that Jennifer best," said Peter. "She's nine but she says she can beat up any kid up to eleven—boy or girl.

I bet she can't get me down, but she's got quite a bit of muscle."

"I liked the Cokes best and the cake best," said Bobby. "I sure drank a lot."

"Yeh," agreed Peter. "They were super. I sure tanked up and so did that Jennifer. Boy! can she drink. We had a contest to see who could take the longest swallow. That girl baby can sure swallow long."

"We got to stay up late, too," said Winthrop.

"I guess it was worth it," said Peter.

"I guess so," said Jamie. "And I didn't scratch a bit, did I, sir?"

"No," I lied agreeably.

"Step—step—slide—" Peter imitated Miss Pettigrew. "Young people! Step—step—slide!"

Winthrop drowsily hummed the "Blue Danube."

And Bobby, who only slept "because it was the law," remarked through a yawn that he wasn't a bit sleepy, leaned his head on my shoulder, and quietly gave himself up to the *status quo.*

CHAPTER FIFTEEN

Men of Letters

It would be oversimplification to say that all days at The Oaks were alike. Weather changed, sports concurred with weather. Marbles and tops popped out of pockets at the right season. Football helmets replaced baseball caps. Wax went onto skis when the nearby mountains turned white. Besides, let the seasons remain static, boys never allow monotony to settle on their environment. However, the routines and schedules of Monday through Friday maintained their unresilient framework, within which the seasons, the days, and the boys achieved their individuality. Only Saturdays and Sundays had different patterns, and even these were rigid in structure.

Sunday's immutable dedication was to two major activities—Chapel in the morning and letter writing in the afternoon. Neither was popular, but Chapel was regarded as riotous carnival compared to letter writing.

Someone once called letter writing a "gentle art." That dewy-eyed dreamer had obviously never visited The Oaks on a Sunday afternoon. Letter writing at The Oaks was certainly not an art—and everything but gentle. It was more of a violent ordeal. For the Junipers and Pines, correspondence was a reluctant duty, but did not constitute the overpowering

165

threat that it did to the Acorns. Some of the older boys actually took pen in hand without mortal struggle. But from the Acorns, letters were as difficult to extract as impacted second molars.

Boys were encouraged to write home any or all days of the week, but they were forcefully coerced into composing letters every Sunday, to fulfill the school's rash pledge to parents that all students would communicate regularly. These were called "home-going letters" and differed from letters dated Monday or Saturday (if there ever were such!) in that they were very much in the nature of an assignment. They were read by the respective dormitory masters, corrected for grammar and spelling, and frequently returned for revision and recopying. Each boy bought his Sunday freedom by delivering a satisfactory letter.

The Acorns, to a man, were obsessed with the physical condition of their loved ones, and seemingly they expected their closest kin to have no curiosity about them beyond a staccato report on the state of glands and metabolism. Spot news reporting had to be forcefully injected into their letters. Spontaneity in the under-ten set almost invariably produced this form letter:

> Dear Mother:
> How are you? I am fine.
> Your loveing son,

Occasionally an ambitious, conscientious boy would stretch the regulation health survey a bit to include fathers, siblings, servants, dogs, cats, and random acquaintances, but the sterility of the letter remained undefiled. Jeffrey presented the following one Sunday:

Dear Mother:
  How are you?
  How is Father?

How is Spot?

How is Fluffy?

How is Miranda?

How is that Mr. Farthingham who delivers the milk that Spot don't like?

I am fine.

> Yours truly,
> *Jeff*

"Put in some news. Tell your mother what you've been doing," was my emphatic plea each week. The boys invariably countered with the empty argument that they had done *absolutely nothing*.

"I haven't done one *single* thing, not one!" Peter insisted one Sunday. This in spite of the fact that at three o'clock when he was corralled for the Ordeal, he was equally strident in arguing that he was much "too busy" to write letters.

"You mean you've been sitting in your room for seven days?"

"No—but I can't say I dressed and went to the bathroom, can I? That's absolutely all I've did."

"Done."

"*Okay*—that's absolutely all I *done*—then."

"Did," I corrected again as a matter of futile habit. "Did you eat?"

"Not very much and it wasn't any good anyway."

"Did you play any games?"

"Oh, I sup*pose* so. But I didn't make a homer or get hurt or anything."

Democracy was beaten to a pulp every Sunday and I handled the knuckle duster. I became a despot—and not a very benevolent one either. I made the laws and administered them, and they were completely devoid of the concept of freedom and equality for all. Bobby Lennox, to whom writing was truly torture, was permitted to get by with a "How-are-you-I-am-fine" job. But Peter and Jamie and Jeffrey were forced to include at least three events in their letters, and there were various standards of regulations for the others. I was Dictator for one hour each week, but I had to fight for my position.

"Go to your room and stay there, Peter, and don't turn on your radio and don't speak to anyone. I don't want to see your face, not once, until you've finished your letter, and I want *three* items in it in no way related to the state of anyone's health."

"Aw, jeeps, sir—what if I have to go to the john?"

"Go now—and avoid such a dire possibility," I suggested.

"Okay—but what if I have to throw up or something?"

"I hereby give you permission to throw up on the floor of your room."

"Who'll clean it up?"

"I will—now go."

"I sure hope I throw up. It would serve you right, too."

"I hope you do, too. Serve you right. Now scram, or I'll bash out your brains." Violent verbiage appealed to the better side of my savages. They always recognized the overtone of tenderness in wild exaggeration and reacted favorably to it. But their reaction time was often a bit prolonged. They played every act far beyond curtain time.

"Yah—then I'd die," Peter said, "and you'd go to jail."

"So—I'm in jail and you're dead. Don't you think we've carried this just about as far as possible?"

Peter frowned thoughtfully and grinned. "Huh-uh—we can still have my funeral, and let them electrocute *you*. That would be fun."

"Madcap fun!" I agreed. "But let's save that for next Sunday's feature attraction. Now beat it."

"Aw heck—" Reluctantly he gave up the struggle and shuffled off to his room.

"Three paragraphs—don't forget," I called after him.

"I heard you the first time," he growled, "and there aren't three facts in the whole wide world, so there." He got the last

word, but I won the round. In half an hour he returned with
his triple-fact letter.

Dear Mother:
  How are you? I am fine.
  I have a mouse. It is not a lady mouse after all. I am sorry. Her name
is George now.
  We went to dancing school. The ones we dance with are girl babies.
They are terrible. The not as terrible one is named Jennifer.
  I need a top off a Wheaties Box. Send quick because this is awfully
important, because I need the badge that you get free.
  I do not want to take violin lessons because my arms get awfully tired
and then I'm worn out and can't do my Arithmetic. Besides, I can play
NOBODY KNOWS HOW DRY I AM real good now, so can't I quit?
  That is three facts now.

                                               Peter

"This is fine, Peter," I said. There was no *double-entendre*
in my praise either. According to our own somewhat unique
criteria for literary achievement, it was an excellent letter.
"Slip in 'love' there, at the end, and you can go and play."

"Heck, I'm too tired to write 'love,'" he said, and sighed
wearily, at the same time purposefully clutching a baseball
in a mitted hand. "I'll just put an *X* and an *O* instead. That
okay?"

"Yes—that will do."

He screwed up his mouth to face the final torture and put
a big *X* in front of his name and a huge *O* after it. Then, as
an afterthought, he decorated the *O* with two dots for eyes
and a nose and a mouth. This embellishment took considerably more time to accomplish than writing "love" would
have.

"I sure write swell letters, don't I? She better appreciate
it too—that's what—or something *terrible* will happen to
her."

"What?" I asked.

"I'll just kill her, that's all," he said cheerfully. He stuck

his baseball cap on his head. "Hey, Jamie!" he shouted. "Bring
your letter and let's go play."

Jamie arrived on the crest of his answering battle cry. "I'm
coming!" He thrust the letter into my hand. "Hurry, please,
we've got so many things to do."

"Well—remember what they were next Sunday, will you?"
I suggested slyly.

I read:

Dear Mother:

I wrote a compsishun. It was about friends. What it was about is that
friends are Okay if they stand up for you.

Mr. Hargrave's dog had puppies. All except one are men. He is a
woman.

My third fact is that I beat up Lance Markham and he's eleven already.
I beat him up for a good cause because he is a stinkpot, so it was okay.

How are you? I am fine.

Your loving son,
James

"Composition's misspelled, Jamie."

"Oh, crap!"

"Try again, Jamie."

"Oh, heck!"

"Better—now I'll erase the word for you and spell it while
you correct. Do you really think Lance Markham is a stinkpot
or would you like to change that, too?"

"Nope—he's a stinkpot all right."

"Yeh—he's a stinkpot, sir," Peter corroborated soberly.

Even under my dedicated dictatorship, I did allow freedom
of opinion its natural rein. Besides, Lance Markham *was* a
stinkpot.

There were a few other rather obligatory letters assigned
to Sunday. Boys who had been entertained over week ends or
during holidays were required to write bread-and-butter notes.
Mrs. Curtis, Homer's mother, was a very kindly person and

almost always invited a boy or two to stay over the week end
at their place. I am not sure her motivation was pure generosity, although it served the same purpose as far as the boys
were concerned. She always coveted a couple of companions
for Homer to distract him from reading the encyclopedia all
week end. Only chess players, however, were invited to the
Curtises.

A happier haven for week enders was Sandy Spencer's home.
He too was a day boy and his family had a ranch near the
school. Mrs. Spencer was a warm, understanding woman who
didn't care whether she did or didn't receive a thank-you
letter for her hospitality, but nevertheless, the boys were required to make the polite gesture.

On one occasion, Peter had been Sandy's guest from Friday
to Sunday noon. "Do I have to write to Mrs. Spencer?" he
demanded. "I already told her I sure had a swell time."

"I know, but it's considered very nice to write a little note
anyway, thanking her. A sentence or two will do."

He went off to accomplish the task. He brought his letter
to me and asked if I wanted to read it. Knowing Mrs. Spencer's compassion for very young letter writers, I told Peter
just to seal the envelope and mail it. He did.

The next day Mrs. Spencer stopped by to see me. She had
the letter in her hand. "See what I got from Peter. Really, it
quite touches me."

I read:

Dear Mrs. Spencer,
    I had a very nice time over the week end. Enclosed please find twenty-
five cents for your cortesy. Respectably yours,
                    Peter Kensington Matthews III

Since Peter was, as Mrs. Spencer knew, on a thirty-five-
cents-a-week spending allowance, his "hostess gift" was truly
lavish. She and I laughed tenderly over the incident. I de-

cided not to have any therapeutic reading with Peter from Emily Post, since his *faux pas* was more than compensated for by his financial sacrifice, which I knew must have postponed for at least another week the current goal of his budgeting. He wanted a turtle very much. Mrs. Spencer knew this, too, and didn't want him deprived. She thanked him profusely for the quarter and then most inoffensively presented him with a turtle, explaining that the poor creature needed a good home.

"Will you take it off my hands?" she asked. "Sandy already has two turtles. I feel the other two are ganging up on this one." Peter was delighted to oblige her.

I made the mistake later of telling Gloria about Peter's *beau geste*. I thought she'd find it amusing and recognize the basic generosity that prompted the gift. On the contrary, Gloria saw nothing humorous in the incident.

"Why, how offensive of Peter," she said. "He knows better than that." In spite of my protests, she reproached him. She explained fully about good breeding and the amenities and pointed out that money was vulgar. The whole recital, however, seemed to wash over Peter like warm water.

He frowned and looked puzzled, and finally said, choosing his words a bit unwisely, it seemed to me, "Well, jeepers, what in heck are you yapping about? I didn't send *you* a quarter, and I promise I never will. But, gee, if I had fifty cents even, I'd sure give it to Mrs. Spencer. She was awful pleased with the quarter."

Gloria shuddered and started all over again, but it was a hopeless crusade.

There was a good deal of innate logic in the Acorns, but still they had no confidence in a possible correlation between letters written and letters received. They loved getting letters. They loved getting mail—any mail—first-class, packages, magazines, second-class, third-class, irrespective of readability. Most of the boys got a few first-class letters each week, of course. They *all* got lots of second-class mail.

This was because they habitually clipped from periodicals any coupons which provided a line for name and a line for address. They rarely bothered to check on what the rewards were to be or just what they were committing themselves to in signing up. Their expectation was that they'd get free samples of something. Sometimes they did get samples. Cluttering up desks were small packets of dyspepsia tablets, toggle bolts, face powder, pieces of plastic, swatches of drapery material, squares of wallboard, vitamin pills, patent medicines, etc. Frequently they got books, trustingly sent out by second-rate publishers with the expectation that five dollars or the book would come back within ten days. I spent a good deal of time tying up such choice items as *The Sex Life of the American Female,* and *How to Write Salable Scenarios.* And I frequently composed elaborate formal letters, explaining that the two-hundred-dollar correspondence course in "Fingerprinting and Other Crime Detection Techniques" didn't quite meet expectations or that the set of all-wool Klondike blankets sent for examination proved to be a bit too heavy for our climate.

But it was impossible to tie up and express back with polite apology plumbing contractors or hopeful insurance agents who had received explicit requests to call on Mr. Kevin Clark or Mr. Peter Matthews to outline a family protection program or check over sanitation needs.

My first encounter with such a disappointed salesman came prior to even a suspicion of my charges' reckless use of the mails. He came to see Kevin. I happened to be in the reception lounge at the time of his arrival and he made his inquiry of me.

"Where will I find Mr. Clark?" he asked. He was a friendly, pleasant-looking man.

"Mr. Clark?" I frowned. "We have no Mr. Clark here," I said, going over in my mind quickly the faculty roster as well as the grounds, stables, and household staff.

"No?" He looked puzzled and checked a slip of paper. "Mr. Kevin Clark?"

"Oh—*Kevin!*" I laughed. I decided he was being a wit and, in addition, it crossed my mind that this might be Kevin's father, the hazy character who had endowed him with his cowlick.

"Are you Mr. Clark?" I asked.

"Me—Mr. Clark? Certainly not. I want to *see* Mr. Clark." He looked slightly worried—about my mental state, no doubt.

"Well—who are you?" I finally demanded forthrightly.

He handed me his card. "I'm Mr. Monteith from the Phoenix office of Allied Insurance. Mr. Clark asked me to call. Are you his secretary?"

"Well, in a manner of speaking—part-time. He doesn't have a full-time secretary. He's only eight, you know."

"*Eight!*" gasped Mr. Monteith. "Eight years old, you mean?"

I was awfully obtuse, of course. I had assumed all the boys were making scrapbooks the day I first observed them feverishly cutting up magazines. That was the sort of thing I did during the more blameless moments of my own childhood. I remember I had landed that day with rejoicing on the little island of uninterrupted peace that their decorous activity provided for me. I had actually spent two joyous hours reading a novel. I should have known there was something counterfeit in such a situation.

Poor Mr. Monteith produced the signed coupon requesting his services by Mr. Kevin Clark. He was a generous man, however, and insisted he had a call to make in Prescott any-

way and that this wasn't more than fifty-five miles out of his
way. I took him over to Joe who always kept in his laundry
bag a precious bottle of Scotch for medicinal purposes or other
emergencies. This seemed a bona fide emergency.

"You mean to tell me, Rosebud," said Joe, "that you don't
check every postcard and letter that leaves your dorm?"

"Of course not," I said. "They have a right to their privacy."

"You don't have to be a nosy sneak about it, but just a casual
inquiring mind does no harm at all. I learned this the hard
way. Marlin Carrington who was a somewhat difficult boy,
as you can surmise from the legends about him that live on
here, once wrote the FBI. He reported that Dr. Barrett was,
in his opinion, a dangerous Russian spy. Well—the FBI always investigates every tip and I found myself in the unhappy
situation of having to swear to the lily-pure character of our
employer. It was hard on me, but I did it. It taught me a
lesson about young males' use of the mails."

Of course, first-class mail—readable messages from friends
and family—had a higher rating than samples or books "in
plain wrappers." I think with many of the boys letters were
even more prized than packages containing catcher's mitts or
caterer's cakes. Certainly to Larry Drummond and Bobby
Lennox, the daily post could produce nothing so valued as
personal letters.

Although these two had the highest pitch of eagerness for
mail, their situations were diametrically different. Larry got
more letters than anyone in the school, and Bobby got fewer.
Both raced to the mail room—one with assurance that what
he expected would be there and one with almost pathological
hope that what he didn't expect would someday miraculously
arrive.

Larry came from a happy, warm family, and he missed
them all very much and they missed him. Besides his sister

Christine at Shadow Creek, he had a sister younger than himself and an older brother at Dartmouth. His parents both wrote him twice weekly—an amazing phenomenon in itself since very few of the boys got actual handwritten letters from their fathers. Even in the most affectionate and conscientious families, most of the letter writing was done by mothers. In addition, Larry's brother and sisters also wrote him regularly and even his uncles and aunts and stray cousins sent him occasional postcards or letters. His family regarded it as a hardship both on Larry and on themselves that it was necessary for him to be away at school when he was only nine. His little sister's letters were not very newsy since she was just six and embarking on the mastery of reading and writing under her mother's tutelage. Her billets-doux were laboriously pencil-printed on stationery decorated with Mother Goose characters.

The rest of the family sent him long, rambling accounts of life at home, but even his little sister's brief messages conveyed the devotion that flavored all the Drummond letters. I remember Larry showed me two of her notes. "Gee," he said proudly. "Isn't it wonderful that my littlest sister, Nance, can write all by herself? Mama used to write letters for her but now she can write to me without anybody helping her except with spelling. See—" He handed them to me. The letters, for all their terse brevity, were tender communications.

Dear Larry: I miss you. I can write. Love from *Nancy*.

Dear Larry: Do not ever get sick. Love from *Nancy*.

Larry nourished himself on his letters and was always in the front line of the mob that stormed the boxes at three o'clock in the afternoon when the daily mail came in.

But just as vigorous an elbower to the front line, and just as eagerly expectant day after day, was Bobby. His eyes never wavered from his own mail cubicle while whatever member of the Pine group assigned to the job, distributed the day's letters. But unlike Larry, he didn't get any letters. He just hoped he would.

It wasn't that his family forgot him. His tuition and his drawing account always came in on time. His father's office manager had specific orders about such things. And just prior to vacations, Mr. Lennox's secretary always wrote Dr. Barrett full instructions on what disposition was to be made of Bobby.

Moreover, his parents telephoned him whenever the whim struck, and they spared no expense. His mother even phoned him once from Bombay, India. I had to get him up out of bed at four o'clock in the morning. He was awfully sleepy at the time and a great many people at the party from which his mother called wanted to get on the line to say hello. She later told me the toll had been something over two hundred dollars, but it was worth it, she said, because everyone got such a kick out of talking to Bobby.

I did not tell her that when her sleep-fogged little son hung up, he said to me, "What was that?" And the next morning at breakfast he related for us a "funny dream" he'd had the night before.

"I was talking on the telephone—see—" he said, "and there was a whole lot of ladies and men kept talking to me and I didn't know any of them and they kept telling me what time it was in Indiana and saying what time was it here? And I didn't know what time it was and then they kept asking me how was I. Sure crazy what you dream."

I explained that it wasn't a dream and that he had actually talked in the night to his mother and some of her friends way out in Bombay, India, not Indiana. He hardly believed it and wasn't much moved by the fact when he finally accepted it.

The older boys, however, were very impressed. "Honest! you actually talked across the transoceanic phone lines, Bob?"

Teddy Lane demanded. "Could you hear well? Say—" he added, "if your mother's in India, how's about saving me some of the stamps off her letters for my collection?"

Bobby was proud of his temporary glory and promised to save *all* his stamps for Ted. From India—from London—from New York—from San Francisco—phone calls came, but no letters.

Generally speaking, Bobby was quite inarticulate on the phone, and merely said "yes" and "no" to what were fairly routine questions from his mother, "Are you trying to get your reading better?"—"Are you being a good boy?" But one night he actually verbalized a whole sentence.

"I was wondering when you were in India if I would get any letters." He paused apologetically. "Because of the stamps, you know. The kids collect stamps out here."

Apparently his mother thought this was a laudable pursuit and two days later a box arrived for Bobby from a Stamp Collectors' Exchange in Los Angeles. In it were vast quantities of small cellophane envelopes with lavish sets of stamps from all over the world. Bobby gave them all to Teddy, who was very grateful.

Bobby went on watching for letters.

I think it was Larry's pride in Nancy's newly acquired ability to write that initiated what became for Bobby a regular custom. Larry showed everyone in the school Nancy's first letter. It covered a large sheet of paper and conveyed only the sentiment, "To Larry. Love from Nancy."

"Want to see what my little sister wrote? She's only six," he asked Bobby.

"Yes," Bobby said eagerly. So he read Nancy's letter.

"Who are those other ones from?" Bobby pointed to the unopened envelopes in Larry's hand.

"From my mother and my father and my brother Hal."

"What does your mother say in her letter?" Bobby asked.

"Come on down to my room and I'll read it out loud to you," Larry offered.

I saw them sitting on Larry's bed and Larry was delivering snatches of the Chronicles of the Drummonds, and making explanatory comments as he read. "We wished you could have been with us on Sunday, darling. We went on a picnic and we missed you so much. Felipe and Amado saddled the horses and went with us. . . ."

"Felipe and Amado. Those are Mexican names, Bobby, and those men work for my father. They're real nice."

"Yeh?—Go on, Larry," Bobby urged.

The next afternoon at three, again Bobby took his front-line stand in the mail room. This time I noticed that he watched not only his own box but also Larry's.

When all the mail was up, he turned to Larry. "Did you get another letter from your mother?"

"Huh-uh, not today, Bob—only from Nance."

"Did you get a letter from *your* mother?" he turned to Winthrop.

"Yeh," said Winthrop.

"Can I go with you and read it, too?" Bobby asked.

"Sure," Winthrop agreed cheerfully. "I'll read it out loud." The boys were all sympathetic with Bobby's reading problem and always covered up for him, even as I did in the classroom.

From then on, Bobby chose a letter each day. The boys all liked Bobby. It gave them a pleasurable feeling of generosity as well as prestige to share their letters with him. They became almost competitive in the matter. "Hey, Bob, you want to read my mom's letter today," someone would yell.

"No—mine's longer, Bob. Come on with me instead. Besides, you read Jeffy's yesterday and Larry's the day before. It's my turn."

Small boys often seem insensitive and heartlessly frank, and certainly the Acorns were no exception. They hurled insults at each other and frequently hurled fists. But none of them was cruel. Even at eight and nine, they seemed to be endowed with some unconscious core of emphatic insight. I worried considerably but I never once heard a boy by so much as a hint imply to Bobby that it was odd that he didn't get any letters of his own. And no one ever pointed out to him that he was squandering both energy and time, pushing himself into the front line at the postboxes every day.

But how far can one trust the tact of a nine-year-old? One day my heart really came up and wooed my epiglottis. Here comes Bobby's knockout blow, I thought. He suddenly revised his routine question, "May I read your letter?"

Instead, he turned to Larry, his face alive with warm eagerness. "Did *we* get a letter?" he asked.

Heaven bless all little boys and reward them with popsicles and catcher's mitts and jackknives and friendly snakes and lots of dirt to wallow in! Larry, with no hesitation, smiled back. "Yep," he said, "*we* got one."

It was this extreme identification with Larry, however, that prompted Joe to take a hand in Bobby's problem. "That poor kid's going to come a cropper," Joe told me. "Bobby has to have a few letters of his own or he's going to forget who he is."

Mrs. Lennox admired Joe very much, and made her feelings odiously obvious, it was my feminine opinion. In fact, my sudden exaggerated dislike for Mrs. Lennox during one of her rare visits forced me to admit to myself that Joe was not a thorn in my side but a song in my heart.

"You wouldn't fall for that female, would you?" I finally asked him.

"Cuddles Lennox, you mean? Why—I think she's utterly charming."

"Oh, Joe! You don't call her 'Cuddles,' do you? Why, she's a vicious, evil, designing old witch!"

"But *so* pretty—" He lifted his chest and sighed.

"Oh, Joe Hargrave! Any woman looks fine with all that pampered grooming and gorgeous clothes, but you just take it from me—"

"You're jealous!" he interrupted. "Why, Cup Cake, your frosting is melting. You're jealous."

"If I'm ever jealous over you, it will be because my brain's come unstuck at the edges." I literally screeched at him— precisely like a woman in love.

Anyway, Joe came to me one day with six stamped, addressed envelopes in his hand. "Say, you feisty little flower, take a gander at these. I'm sending them to Cuddles, with a covering note of instructions. I've typed them. All she has to do is sign "Mama" and drop these letters in the box once a week. It's high time Bobby got a letter of his own."

I read the letters. They were exactly right. You'd have thought Joe had been a mother for twenty years.

"Oh, Joe, they're wonderful, but what will Barrett say?"

"He'll say that the letter he sent Mrs. Lennox six months ago, suggesting she write to Bobby, has finally borne fruit."

"But will she send the letters? Maybe she'll be mad," I suggested.

"Nonsense, Simple, you forget that Cuddles and I understand each other. Besides, if you think these letters are good, you should read the one I wrote to Mama. It would triphammer the heart of an ice maiden. Want to read it?"

"*No!*"

The device worked.

Three days later, Bobby was keeping vigil at his usual post. But he no longer watched his own box. His eyes were glued on Larry's cubicle. All of a sudden, Tim McNeill, who was distributing mail, let out a shout. *"Bobby!* You got a letter! You got a letter, Bobby."

Slowly Bobby held up both hands, like a cherub in supplication. Tim put the envelope into them.

"It's got my name on it," Bobby announced incredulously. Then he cried out, "I got one myself! I got a letter! Hey guys! Anyone want to read my letter?"

"Yes"—"Yes"—"You read it, Bobby. Read it!" It was chorus.

"I guess I can read it myself," he said in a thin voice, and ripped open the envelope.

"Sure you can read it," Tim reassured him. He lifted him up on the counter in front of the mailboxes, and put the rest of the mail aside. All the boys gathered around.

" 'Dearest Son' " he began haltingly. "I can't read so very fast," he apologized.

"That's okay, Bob, try and read it *real* slow. It's better slow so we can hear every word," Larry said.

So Bobby read his letter *"real* slow" so they could hear every word. No mother ever wrote a nicer letter to her little boy.

CHAPTER SIXTEEN

A Birthday

"I'LL never forget the day you were born." I imagine that Joseph Leonard Jorgenson has, throughout the years, often heard people speak of his birthday with an overtone of regret. Of course, he undoubtedly knows and understands why the appropriate jubilation which marked the morning of his birthday was displaced by nightfall with tragic grief.

Mrs. Jorgenson left the school a month before her baby was due to arrive and stayed with friends in Prescott. This somewhat prolonged precaution was to alleviate Dr. Barrett's fearful anxiety that the child might, by some awful catastrophe of mistiming, be born on the premises. Also, there was the realistic possibility that a last-minute frantic drive to the hospital might prove hazardous in the uncertain weather of February. Mr. Jorgenson stayed on at The Oaks to teach his classes, with nervous distraction, during the weeks of waiting.

Each morning when the boys came into the dining room for breakfast, they immediately checked Mr. Jorgenson's place to see if he'd been summoned in the night. Although the impending event was delicately avoided in table conversation, in deference to Dr. Barrett, the boys were almost as excited as Mr. Jorgenson.

The Pines, under Joe's supervision, redecorated the walls

183

of the small bedroom in the Jorgenson cottage which was to become the nursery. And my little Acorns devoted their Arts and Crafts for several weeks to building and painting a wooden train for the baby.

"In case you don't know," Kevin broke the news to me gently, "Mrs. Jorgenson's going to get a baby."

"Yeh, that's why she's fat," Peter added the scientific detail. "So we're making him a train."

"Did it ever occur to you boys," demanded Homer, with some logic, "that this child may be female?"

"Sez you!" Peter scoffed.

"He means it might be a girl, Pete. It could be, you know." Larry reluctantly sided with Homer. "My sister Nancy was a girl. We *could* get a girl this time, too."

Their anticipation was identical with that of a large family of children eagerly awaiting a new sibling.

"One of Mr. Hargrave's puppies was a woman—remember?" Bobby pointed out. "She was a real good bitch though."

"I tell you what," suggested Jamie. "Let's us make a cradle for a doll, too, just in case something awful does happen."

"Nope, that's dopey," Peter said. "It's pretty sure to be a boy and then the cradle would be wasted. Why don't we make a sled instead, because boys' sleds and girls' sleds are exactly alike."

"Did it ever occur to you," demanded Homer once more, "that this neonate—whether female *or* male—will be absolutely incapable of using either a train or a sled? I suggest we make a rattle."

"Aw crap!" Winthrop attacked Homer. "This baby is not going to be either male or female, see—it's going to be a girl or a boy, and we're going to make a sled."

"And what's more, Homer Curtis," Peter said decisively, "I betcha this will be a real smart kid—look how quick Mr.

Jorgenson can do arithmetic problems and everything—and besides, with all of us to teach him stuff, he'll get on to things. He'll want a sled."

Thursday the sky was heavy with leaden clouds and by midafternoon the range of white-topped mountains to the north stood out like chalked diagrams on a blackboard. The boys kicked up their heels like corralled colts.

"It's going to snow! It's going to snow!" they trumpeted the tidings. "Tomorrow we can go sledding! Tomorrow we can ski!"

At dinnertime the electricity failed and we ate by candlelight. Candlelight is conceded to be flattering to women, but it does something equally enchanting to little boys—and to big boys, too. Joe sat at the opposite end of my table. It crossed my mind that I'd never seen anyone who looked nicer by candlelight than Joe. The flame and shadow emphasized the rugged bone structure and also the gentle tenderness of his face. And the little boys might have been cherubs by Botticelli. Men of all ages object to candlelight at dinnertime except when the utilities fail, so I had to take advantage of my rare opportunity. I kept my eyes open during grace for the pleasure of looking at the bowed heads and the softly moving lips—"Our Father, we thank Thee for this food—" Angels!

However, I noted that Jeffy had his eyes open, and was frankly counting the cinnamon rolls on the fingers of his supposedly sacredly folded hands. And Bobby was rubbing his fist across his forehead in an effort to mop up the moisture dripping from his hair. He had, as usual, splashed it with water at the last minute when he couldn't find his comb. And Jamie had his eyes tightly closed and his face was a contorted caricature. He was making another valiant effort to wear wool, and with his fingers spread like claws, he was scratching his

flanneled legs with both hands. Winthrop was slyly poking
Larry with a fork.

Of course, I couldn't reprove any of them, since "eyes
closed" was our rule of prayer. . . . "Amen."

"Amen, there's two apiece and one left over. I got wackies
on it!" Jeffrey announced in a single breath.

The usual argument followed. I often wondered how well
fed boys have to be to forego willingly their atavistic attitude
toward food. It took something more traumatic than subdued
lights to subdue dinner noises.

In the middle of the meal, Mr. Jorgenson got his call.
Rosita summoned him to the kitchen phone. The boys stopped
eating. Some of them froze with their forks halfway to their
mouths. The whole dining hall became as quiet as an empty
room while every boy strained to hear the conversation on the
kitchen extension. When Mr. Jorgenson returned, he looked
exactly like a frenzied young man about to become a father.
He spoke in a whisper to Dr. Barrett.

Dr. Barrett arose and made his veiled announcement. "Mr.
Jorgenson has been called to Prescott on some business and
will probably be away for a day or so."

"My gosh, sir!" Peter interrupted. "He's not going down
to Prescott on business. He's going to have a baby. Didn't you
know?"

This broke the conspiracy of silence into tinkling laughter,
and once the dignity had been lightly dropped, it began
crashing all over the room. The older boys burst into loud,
masculine guffaws.

Even Dr. Barrett smiled. "Thank you, Peter," he said. "You
know, I did suspect that there was something unusual about
this trip. Let's all wish Mr. Jorgenson well."

Teddy Lane started singing, "For he's a jolly good fellow,"
and everyone joined in. James and Joe left to warm up the

car and put on the chains while Mr. Jorgenson packed his
bags.

Joe came back very shortly to suggest to Dr. Barrett that
probably one master, or preferably two, should accompany
Leonard, since the snow was falling heavily and certainly no
plows could be expected on the highway until morning. "They
may have to shovel their way," he said.

Dr. Barrett frowned. "It will disorganize our Friday schedule badly with three masters gone."

"Well, if the baby is born tonight or tomorrow as predicted,
and if the weather clears, as predicted—why don't we pro-
claim Friday a celebration day and take the boys up White
Mountain to ski?" Joe suggested. "Besides—someone will *have*
to go with Jorgenson. The guy's too pregnant to drive."

Wallace and James went, leaving Joe and Munsey, the two
skiing experts, to supervise the home front, backed up by
Marcus, a mediocre but willing winter sportsman.

The next day the world was white but surrounded with a
sparkling blue sky. The boys all tramped into breakfast in
ski boots, just in case the predictions came to pass.

"I have an announcement to make." Dr. Barrett spoke
warmly. It seemed to relax him to know that the boys had all
accepted the facts of life and that he no longer need guard
them as classified material. "This morning at six o'clock I
had a phone call from Mr. Jorgenson. He has a son who has
been named 'Joseph Leonard Jorgenson.' I can't imagine why
they'd name him *Joseph!*"

"Oh, sir!" Kevin spoke up boldly. "They named him for
Mr. Hargrave. I'd do the same thing."

"He knows it, Stupe," Peter sneered. "That's a joke. He'd
do the same thing, too."

"How does it feel to be immortalized, Hargrave?" Munsey
asked.

"I can die in peace now," Joe said.

And everyone laughed.

Everyone kept on laughing. Snow. Holiday from school. A new baby. A sparkling day. The skis and sleds were strapped onto the tops of the station wagons, and thermos jugs and sandwich baskets were stowed under the seats. The snowplows had cleared the highway. Joe drove the car in which the Acorns and I were assigned.

We sang all the way to the mountain—"Hector, the Garbage Collector," and "Old Dan Tucker," and "You Can't Get to Heaven in a Rocking Chair."

"You know, sir—" Peter finally broke into the singing to speak soberly to me. "I just thought of something simply super. If you were to marry Mr. Hargrave, you could have some babies, too."

"Yeh—wouldn't that be wizard?" Bobby added. "And then you could buy a great big house to keep them in and maybe all of us could come and live there with you, too."

"Sure! We could do errands and stuff like that for our keep and since you are teachers, none of us would have to go to school ever again. Oh boy!" Jamie suggested.

"Maybe Mr. Hargrave doesn't feel any biological urge in connection with you, sir," Homer speculated flatteringly.

"Oh, I don't know, Homer. We might get around that someway. At least *I* never call her 'sir,' " Joe said. "How's about it, Winsome? People name babies for me, remember? I'm pretty wonderful—want to marry me?"

"Thank you so much, but I'm saying no for the last time."

"Oh gee, sir, I'd grab him if I were a dame," Peter advised me in loud voice from the back seat.

"She is grabbing me," Joe said. "She's just closing in subtle-like. You noticed, she definitely said she was saying no for the *last* time. So—I'll ask her tomorrow again and then she'll say 'yes.' " He paused and his voice dropped. "Will you?" He was really asking.

"Yes," I said—and I was really answering.

Winthrop sat between us on the front seat. Joe reached across him and clasped my hand in his for a brief moment. "Kiss her for me, Winthrop," he said.

"Aw gee, sir—she's sure okay and everything, but—gee!"

"You don't have to kiss her, Winthrop," Homer advised sensibly. "That was merely a figure of speech. He'll do it later. It wouldn't affect her glands a bit if *you* did it."

The romantic overtones of this moment seemed to leave the Acorns quite unmoved. "Want to hear a *real* dirty story?" Peter changed the subject.

"Certainly *not!*" I complied as expected.

"Oh well, I'll tell it anyway. There was a white horse and he rolled in the mud. Get it?" Everyone did.

Lots of other people had the same idea that we did about White Mountain. The long run was already alive with flashing streaks of color and at the base of the hill the powdery snow flew up in brief clouds as the experts spun around in their final Christys.

The boys pummeled out of the station wagons and immediately started chasing each other with handfuls of snow. Joe and Munsey and Marcus collected them, divided them in groups, and assigned them to their skiing areas, according to their abilities. My boys were all in the novice class.

"I'll run down the big one once," Joe said, "and then I'll come over and work with the Acorns. Munsey, you and Marc can have the old-timers today."

We watched Joe's progress up the tow. At the top, he paused, waved his poles at us, poised himself like a bird, and then swooped down the slope, swaying and turning, leaning on the wind with expert grace.

"You looked like you had wings, sir," Kevin said when Joe swirled to a stop.

"Well—I haven't and the chances are I'll be a long time in getting a pair."

All morning he worked patiently with the Acorns on the short slope. Some of the older boys came over from time to time to ask him technical advice. Joe was our best skier and most experienced mountain man. I wish he hadn't been.

At noon we gathered in the Forest Service shelter in front of the fire for lunch. The boys gulped down the hot soup and short-circuited the sandwiches.

"Peanut butter is sure the best stuff that was ever invented," Bobby announced. The observation seemed sage to me. The peanut butter tasted wonderful. Everything tasted wonderful. Even the air had a tangy taste. The burning pinion logs smelled like incense. Laughter drifted skyward with the smoke.

This is the happiest day I have ever known, I thought.

A scream from the high wall of granite mountain to the left suddenly splintered our laughter. Joe leaped to his feet and dashed across the forest clearing. "Stay there, everybody," he yelled back.

Very shortly he returned on the run. "Get our ropes, Munsey," he called. "There's a high-school boy from Phoenix halfway up that cliff. He and two other kids were hiking up on the ridge and got too close to the edge. They don't know anything about snow. The drifts are deceiving up there. He went right through and over, but thank God, caught himself on a ledge. We'll have to go up for him and also rescue the other two. They're marooned by their fright on the top." The men talked as they collected their gear.

"Can't we take the trail to the ridge and lower a rope to the kid? We can pull him up," Munsey suggested.

"No, he's hurt apparently, and that's a jagged cliff."

"Oh?" Munsey hesitated. "It'll be tough going, Joe."

"Yes, I know. But there's plenty of expert help here today." He turned to me. "You and Marc take the boys back to school. You can pack them into two cars. Leave us one station wagon, and call the Highway Department. We may need an ambulance."

"Joe!" I put my hand over my mouth to hold in my fright.

"Don't worry, darling. Take care of the boys."

"I will, Joe."

We never kissed each other.

I finally got all the Acorns dunked and rubbed down but not quieted down. The excitement of the day still had them pitched high. I herded them into my sitting room for chocolate and cookies in front of the fire. They finally relaxed and listened sleepily while I read them a chapter from *Quo Vadis,* a book highly recommended by Dr. Barrett, and which I reserved for sedation purposes. Once their manic state became quiescent, I gave them their freedom until dinner.

Most of them had gone down to the shop to finish painting little Joe's new sled when Bob Munsey appeared at my door.

Kevin was still in my room and so were Winthrop and Larry. Munsey looked like a battle-weary, gray-faced viking in his muddy disheveled ski clothes. He did not greet us. He stood framed in the doorway a moment and then strode purposefully toward Kevin who was lying on my sofa reading a comic book.

Kevin pulled his sprawled legs and arms together and stood up quickly. He was still afraid of Munsey. Larry and Winthrop paused in their checker game on the floor.

"Kevin." Munsey's voice seemed to choke on his words. "I've never apologized for what I did to you once. I'm a big, blundering jackass. I hope you'll forgive me. Every Saturday between now and Commencement, I'll give you boxing lessons."

Larry and Winthrop were no less startled than I. And Kevin's lower jaw looked as if it had lost its articulation. Little boys aren't well schooled in how to handle humility in grownups.

Kevin blushed and stammered. "Why—that's—that's okay, sir. It sure is okay. Gee—it doesn't matter. I shouldn't have hit you that time."

"Yes, you should have," Munsey said. "Will you boys please leave now?"

"Yes, sir." Winthrop and Larry, neither normally alert to obey, spoke in chorus and leaped to their feet to follow Kevin's quick exit. At the door, however, Larry paused momentarily in his eager flight. "Say, sir," he asked, "did Mr. Hargrave save that kid?"

"Yes, he saved him."

"Swell!" They went galloping down the corridors to spread the good news.

Munsey closed the door and then stood with his back against it. His great shoulders suddenly started shaking and his face crumbled into shapeless pain.

"Why, Bob?" I suddenly didn't hate him. He seemed a child who had lost his defenses and stood before me in complete vulnerability. I walked over to him and, as if he were Kevin in a nightmare, I put my arms around him. "Something has happened to you—"

"Yes. Something has happened to all of us."

And then fear put a cold finger on me. I clutched Munsey's arm. "Where's Joe?"

"Joe is dead."

CHAPTER SEVENTEEN

In Memory

THE boy that Joe rescued was named Henry Smith. He had a broken arm, a sprained ankle, and minor skin lacerations when Joe reached him. He was later more seriously cut and bruised while being pulled up the jagged mountainside.

Joe, secure with a rope manipulated by Munsey, managed to work himself down the face of the cliff to the narrow ledge where Henry Smith lay. He removed the rope from himself and fashioned it into a sling harness for the boy. Munsey lowered a second rope to Joe. But before it reached him, the weight of the two overburdened their narrow shelf of safety. The rocks beneath them gave way. One was suspended in space, but saved by his rope sling. One plunged on down the white, deceptively soft-looking surface of the cliff. That was Joe.

There is no one simple way to meet grief, no optimal manner of mourning, no single expression of bereavement. And there is no magic micrometer to measure human suffering. Most of us adopt disguises for our desolation and no one ever sees the full stark face of pain. We at The Oaks were no exception. I know I masqueraded in strength for the sake of the Acorns. And Dr. Barrett wore the mask of calm acceptance. Munsey sobbed as he related the afternoon's tragedy, and Dr.

Barrett's only comment was "This is exceedingly regrettable, but you must pull yourself together, Munsey."

He called all the boys into the lounge to tell them what had happened. Resentment stained the purity of my grief. Why should this man be alive and Joe dead? And being alive, why should he arise with cool competence to evaluate Joe's life for these boys that Joe had loved? Let Roger Frane speak of his friend—or let Marcus Carson, obviously shattered, bring words out of his stricken heart.

But the pomposity and glibness that I expected from Dr. Barrett were missing in his speech. Not only the boys but the masters and I leaned forward to listen to his halting words.

". . . So he is gone. He died saving a boy named Smith. I am glad some way that the boy's name was Smith—Henry Smith. There are hundreds of boys in America named Henry Smith. So—in a way, this boy is symbolic of all boys, and even in dying, our friend, Joe Hargrave, made the final commitment to his personal philosophy which was that every boy is worth while—worth saving."

Dr. Barrett paused to rein in his tugging emotions. His mask was slipping. I realized that I had never until this moment seen the best of Dr. Barrett, just as I had never seen the best of Munsey until this dreadful day.

Jamie broke into the silence. "Would Mr. Hargrave be in heaven by now, sir?" he asked. All my little Acorns strained for his answer. Heaven is an important concept to small boys. I remember how they worried when one of Joe's pups died, for fear that St. Peter might not be a dog lover.

"Jamie." Dr. Barrett cleared his throat and continued. "We don't know much about heaven. I don't think we're supposed to know. But we do know something of one kind of immortality. Joe Hargrave is part of the fabric of all our lives and, therefore, we have not really suffered a final loss of him. He did much more for *us,* you know, than he did for

Henry Smith. As you grow older and have the strength to be tender, the wisdom to laugh, the compassion to be tolerant, and the integrity to speak truth—this great man will be alive in you."

Again he paused, and when he continued I realized that he was no longer addressing the boys, but the faculty.

"As I direct this school in the future, I shall try with warmth and sincerity to consider each boy and each teacher as a dignified individual with a unique constellation of human values and human needs. Then Joe will be living in *me*, too. I hope you will all help me."

Marcus, sitting beside me, lifted his head and turned toward me. The pain in his eyes seemed palliated. "He *means* it," he whispered to me. "Damned if the old boy doesn't!"

"He has half the deed done," Roger spoke aloud, "who has made a beginning. Horace said that almost two thousand years ago."

That night the Acorns undressed promptly, hung up their clothes, and brushed their teeth without being coerced. Then, in their slippers and robes, they gathered as usual in my room. I was sitting on my couch and Kevin and Jeffrey came and sat very close to me, one on each side. Bobby, with no apology, crawled onto my lap, and Winthrop and Larry and Peter and Jamie sat on the floor as near to my knees and to each other as they could. They were very quiet. We were an affectionate huddle, communicating sympathy and mutual support to each other in silence. I think the Acorns were as eager to give me comfort me as I was to succor them.

Finally Larry spoke. "Do you suppose, sir, that Henry Smith, that kid that Mr. Hargrave saved, will turn out to be the President of the United States and free some slaves somewhere or like that, maybe?"

"Or maybe he'll get to be the greatest doctor in the whole world," Peter suggested, "and cure leprosy and all kinds of awful diseases and stuff."

They were groping for a pattern, a purpose, or justification for our loss.

"I been wondering"—Bobby chose his words carefully—"if whenever someone gets born, God makes somebody die. And because that Jorgenson baby got named for Mr. Hargrave, maybe God picked him."

"Nope, Bobby! God's not *that* type," Kevin protested. "But that little baby Joe—maybe *he'll* grow up and be real great. You think so, sir?"

"He may," I said, "but you're the boys who really knew Joe. Henry Smith won't ever forget him, but he didn't really know him, and little Joe never even saw him. You're the fortunate ones. You'll remember him always. But it's not a matter of becoming a great doctor or a president." Barrett had said it all, and better. "Remember what the headmaster said—it's a matter of becoming men who are unselfish, gentle, honest, and brave."

"You know what—" Peter sounded utterly astonished. "You *know*—I'm kinda glad we didn't put all those moths in Dr. Barrett's closet, after all. He's not so bad, is he?"

"Gee, you never know who to hate for sure, do you, sir?" Kevin said, and I knew he was pondering over Munsey rather than Barrett.

"I guess when you really get to know somebody, you don't hate him," Larry said. "I remember one time I saw Lance Markham crying like everything, and he told me he was crying because nobody liked him. You know, I said, 'Aw gee, I like ya,' and I *did* sort of."

"I think Larry's right," I said.

Bobby wiggled around on my lap. "You know what, I think we ought to make a wreath or something."

"Yep," Peter agreed. "After all, we made a train for the baby and we don't even *know* him."

"And Winthrop can write real swell poems—practically the best poems in the whole wide world. Shouldn't Winthrop help us write a poem?" Bobby added.

"Let's do it right now," Kevin said. "Oh, heck, sir, I suppose it's too late?"

It was past bedtime already and they had had a long, difficult day. Still, activity might help them.

"You may stay up as late as you like," I told them.

"We don't have any flowers though," Jamie said.

"We can draw them with crayons," Peter suggested. "I'll show you."

They ran off down the corridor, and they were chattering and arguing again. I was glad.

I wanted to cry, but knew I'd better postpone my tears until they were all asleep.

In about an hour they returned with a large cutout of a wreath. It was decorated with every color in the Crayola box, and obviously both the best and poorest artists had contributed to the total effect. Most of the flowers were at least distant kin to the daisy family. Pasted across the wreath was a narrow strip of paper carefully printed with the legend, REST IN PEACE. Attached to the bottom was Winthrop's ode:

> *In Memory*
> Good-by, Mr. Hargrave, we're sorry you went.
> You were a awful wonderful gent.
>
> From the Acorns

The wreath showed the usual dark smudges from thumbs, characteristic of all *pièces d'art* pasted by little boys.

"Isn't this wreath just *beautiful?*" Bobby said.

"Yes, it is," I agreed.

"I betcha he'll sure like it," Peter said. "Won't he? And the poem, too."

"Yes, he'll *love* them both." It was the one thing about which I was absolutely sure.

It would be a happy-ever-aftermath of our tragedy to be able to say that Dr. Barrett and all the boys and masters dedicated themselves henceforth to lofty and noble deeds. This was, of course, not the case.

Still, in Dr. Barrett's struggle between bigotry and tolerance, bigotry was losing ground. And although Munsey still wore his arrogance, it seemed a bit too snug for his size. Also, I noticed that my little boys *very* occasionally restrained their fists to give judicial consideration before plowing into their "enemies." Brotherly love's progress was pretty slow. The most startling and consistent change affected by our traumatic experience came where I least expected it. Regularly, twice a week, Bobby got a letter from his mother, not typewritten, but in her own hand.

There was not much to imply deep shifting of channels in the life of the school, and at times Joe seemed forgotten. Marcus and I both decided that we would not return to The Oaks the following year. I had a chance for a job in California, and Marcus decided to sell his land and take a trip around the world.

"After all—what difference will it make if this place has five fewer oaks next year?" he said.

Then Commencement crept up on us.

Throughout the year certain events on the school calendar took on a mild touch of saturnalia. Our high points of madcap festivity were the Halloween and April Fool's Day parties (both subtly designed to leash rather than license boyish enthusiasm), the annual dance for the Shadow Creek girls, the Christmas party, and the spring horse show. All these headline events involved lengthy preparation and dramatic presentation.

But they all paled into significance compared to the pomp

and pageantry of Commencement. This was Dr. Barrett's final *coup de théatre*—his most ostentatious stratagem for recapturing the boys for the following fall term.

Weeks ahead of time, the choir began rehearsing. "The tumult and the shouting dies—" (I began praying that it would!) "The captains and the kings depart—" (Oh, speed the day!) The saintly purity of boys' voices is one of life's magnificent ironies. More deviltry than angelic dedication is contrived behind hymnals, I am sure.

All the students were herded together daily to learn by interminable practice the laborious gait of the Commencement march. The boys who were not slated to play a violin or piano solo memorized recitations. Of course—and alas!— the boys slated to play violin and piano solos also put in extra practice hours.

It was part of Dr. Barrett's faultless technique to have every boy perform on the program. It was the one day of the year when almost all parents put in an appearance. And irrespective of the toll it took in teacher time and disposition, every parent had his own personal reward at Commencement.

A mother with one child slated for public performance can usually, without suffering schizophrenia, engineer him through his memory work. However, by the time every one of my Acorns knew "his piece," I myself couldn't have remembered "Roses are red, violets are blue—"

The grooming for Commencement also involved me strenuously. All boys had to be taken to town for haircuts. Clothes had to be cleaned and almost as many new purchases had to be made as for dancing school. On the morning of the grand finale, I had to supervise the dressing of the Acorns to be sure that they were properly scrubbed and polished and attired in white pants, white shirts, and school jackets. That was mild warm-up, however. My real challenge came with the subsequent struggle to maintain my victory over dirt and disorder

until two o'clock. The odds were against me, of course, and
there were invariably last-minute emergency repairs of the
ravages worked by boy and Nature.

Eventually, however, not only all the parents arrived but
two o'clock arrived. The audience sat on stiff folding chairs
on the lawn and our grand spectacle was staged on an im-
provised platform.

What a struggle, I thought. Weeks of agony so that each
set of parents may for five minutes glow with pride when
their own child ornaments them by playing a tortured version of "Londonderry Air" or recites, without a flicker of
feeling and at a madly accelerated speed, "Abou ben Adhem,
may his tribe increase—"

Precisely like his procedure on opening day, Dr. Barrett
assigned us to our battle stations. Certain parents were our
designated responsibility. I drew Mr. and Mrs. Phillip Standish (formerly Clark, etc., Byrne-Masterson) and the Bannisters. I sat between the two women. Mrs. Lennox sat in front of
me. I was very tired and they looked very rested and expensive
to me. I decided I didn't like them.

Then while we awaited the first chord of the overture, Mrs.
Lennox turned around and spoke to me. "Have you by any
chance read any of my letters to Bobby?"

"Why, yes," I answered. "As a matter of fact, Bobby often
reads them aloud to all of us."

"Are they all right?" she whispered, and there was breathless urgency in her voice. "I am trying awfully hard."

"They're fine," I assured her.

"He's just a little boy, and I don't know him very well,"
she continued. "I'm sort of a stupid person. I wish you could
tell me things about him, because my husband and I have
talked it over and we've decided not to send him to camp
this summer. We're just going to stay home and sort of get
acquainted with him. It scares me." She paused. "By the way,

we're awfully sorry about Mr. Hargrave. He was quite a remarkable person."

What was it Kevin had said? "You never know who to hate
for sure, do you?"

"I'll tell you everything I possibly can about Bobby," I said.

The music started. Mrs. James played the piano. The choir
led the processional, wearing their vestments and carrying
their open books. For once, not one of the reluctant songsters
was giggling, nor was anyone kicking the heels of the boy
ahead of him. Andy Mansfield, who was our most talented
alto, was actually singing in full voice. He often went mute
on us and just moved his mouth for the satisfaction of hearing all the other altos lose their pitch without his support.
They all looked proud and intense. They were taking this
seriously. Perhaps the struggle aught availeth, after all.

> The tumult and the shouting dies—
> The captains and the kings depart—

My spine began to tingle. "Lest we forget—lest we forget—"

Of course, some of the boys did forget—their lines! But
still, the recitations were eventually all recited and the musical
renditions all rendered. Kevin, pushing back his cowlick,
bowed stiffly, sat down at the piano and polished off for the
last time, I hope, the "Minuet in G." He played it at break-
neck speed, without a single pause.

"Why, he's doing awfully well, isn't he?" his mother whispered to me. "But I see you didn't break him of that horrible
habit."

"Yes, he's doing beautifully," I agreed. "And none of his
habits are horrible."

Finally, Dr. Barrett arose and presented the awards and the
diplomas.

"To Timothy Marston McNeill, member of the Pines, and
a graduating student, I present the Headmaster's Trophy for

the boy who in character and accomplishment best represents the school—"

"To Homer William Curtis, member of the Acorns, I present the Chadwick Trophy for highest scholastic achievement—" Well—naturally.

"To Robert Millbank Lennox, Acorn, I present the Smedley Award for most outstanding scholastic progress—" The worst reader in the third grade—it was wonderful! Of course, his collar was turned up and touching his right ear and his tie was offside when he marched up for his honor, but I was as proud as if I had personally invented him. I found it necessary to dab at my eyes.

Dr. Barrett delivered his Commencement message to the boys and parents. His speech followed his usual formula— "Onward and upward, etc.—" but now and then he paused and it occurred to me that he was getting bored with his own banalities and that next year he very well might write a new graduation address. I wondered what he'd say.

That afternoon when I said good-by to the Acorns, Bobby asked me the question: "You'll be waiting for us when we get back here next September, won't you, sir?"

Peter gave my answer for me, and I accepted it. "What a silly thing to ask, Dopey," he said. "Of course, she'll be here. Where would she go?"

That was a good question. I could think of lots of places to go—but curiously enough, no place I'd rather go.